About Franz

C. G. Jung's Tower House Retreat, Böllingen, Switzerland

About Franz

Remembering C. G. Jung—A Son's Story

Mary Dian Molton

with Janet Sunderland

SHANTI ARTS PUBLISHING
BRUNSWICK, MAINE

About Franz: Remembering C. G. Jung—A Son's Story

Published by Shanti Arts Publishing
Cover and interior design by Shanti Arts Designs

Shanti Arts LLC
Brunswick, Maine
www.shantiarts.com

Printed in the United States of America

Cover image and frontispiece — C. G. Jung's Tower House Retreat, Böllingen by Andrew Taylor, 2009. Creative Commons. Wikimedia Commons

Photographs on pages 10–13 were taken by the author and used with her permission.

ISBN: 978-1-951651-70-1 (softcover)
ISBN: 978-1-951651-71-8 (digital)

Library of Congress Control Number: 2021934191

For Warren, my beloved spouse of seventy years,
and our whole wide family that followed
from that first date, New Year's Eve, 1949.

ACKNOWLEDGMENTS

This book began with a knock on a door in Zurich, Switzerland, and the invitation to lasting friendship that followed. Since then, I've been the beneficiary of many efforts, large and small, that have been invaluable to the book's completion.

For their generosity, their good will, their candor and trust, I would like to thank Franz's companion, Els Glaser, and Franz Jung himself. For their patient and continuous critique and editorial perspective over years of careful consideration, my gratitude to Jennifer Molton, Stephen Molton, Warren Molton, Pamela Galvin, and Bruce Kellogg. And, through the insight of David Molton, my thanks flow to our longtime family friend and colleague, the late Carol Porteous, for her painstaking and heartfelt editing at a critical turning point in the book's evolution.

To them, to my dear and discerning grandsons, Aaron and Eric Siemers, to our intrepid Jessica Molton and a squad of computer rescuers, and to every other person who offered technical expertise or simply their kind words of curiosity and support, I am ever grateful.

Mary Dian Molton

CONTENTS

PART ONE

This story began in Küsnacht, Switzerland, and may possibly last as long as interest remains in the work and family of Franz Jung's illustrious father, Carl Gustav Jung.

PART TWO

I am re-entering this project late in my life because it doesn't leave me to rest in peace without bringing this story of Franz Jung and Els Glasser to its ultimate conclusion.

Franz and Mary Dian in Franz's living room in Küsnacht, Switzerland

A wintry view of the town of Küsnacht, Switzerland

A view of the Böllingen Tower from the lake

People lined up to enter Böllingen

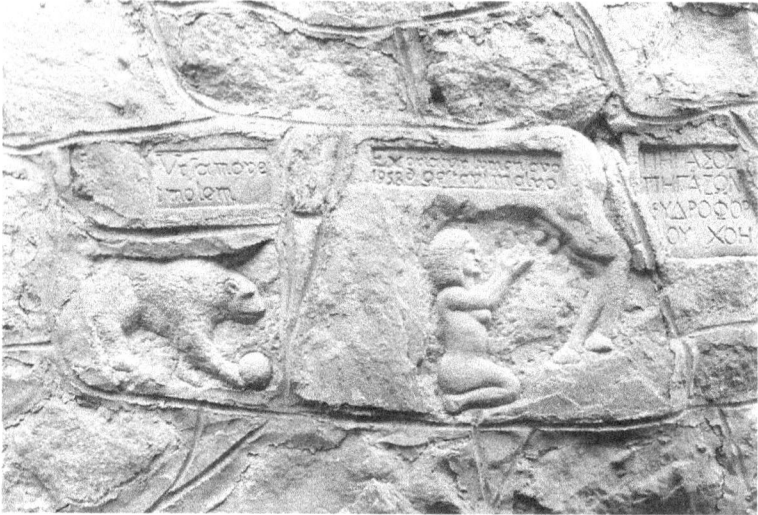

Carving by C. G. Jung

Carving by C. G. Jung

Carving by C. G. Jung. Translation: "I am an orphan, alone yet encountered everywhere, single yet opposed to myself, young and old at the same time, neither father nor mother did I know, for I am to be raised from the depth in likeness of the Fish, or I descend from heaven like the White Stone, through groves and mountains do I wander, yet I hide in innermost man, am mortal within every single head, and still am not touched by the changing of the seasons."

Carving by C. G. Jung. Translation: "Time is a child playing like a child playing a board game the kingdom of the child. This is Telesphoros, who roams through the dark regions of this cosmos and glows like a star out of the depths. He points the way to the gates of the sun and to the land of dreams."

PART ONE

This story began in Küsnacht, Switzerland, and may possibly last as long as interest remains in the work and family of Franz Jung's illustrious father, Carl Gustav Jung. The pieces rested on ragged pages, sets of letters, notebooks, and dusty journals stored for more than thirty years in a battered suitcase at the back of my office closet. My family members and I referred to it as the "monster in the closet."

CHAPTER ONE

MEETING FRANZ JUNG

❋

MY LIFE WAS FULL. I MAINTAINED OUR HOUSEHOLD, EARNED VARIOUS university credentials, taught school, developed a therapy practice, and co-authored and published *Four Eternal Women*, a book based on the work of Toni Wolff, a colleague and associate of Carl Jung. But the "monster" began to poke at me, and it gradually emerged in bits, pieces, and dreams, all of which led me to pull out the suitcase and arrange the preliminary material chronologically by year on a table in my study, beginning with 1988, the year I met Franz Jung, and ending eight years later at the time of his death in 1996.

The tangled pieces from which the story grew are very old as I am now in my eighties. But they began to coil around each other as far back as 1978 when my husband, Warren, and I were present at our first two-week seminar at the C. G. Jung Institute in Küsnacht, Switzerland. The seminars were led by the Institute's superb faculty members between academic semesters and during vacation times for the benefit of Jungian enthusiasts who came from all over the world. These many years later, when I become frustrated, feeling this story of Franz is an insurmountable task with papers and notes strewn about, I think of my notes as coaxing me for attention to my early times when I managed to attend seminars at the C. G. Jung Institute.

Warren and I shared a long and mutual interest in Carl Jung's analytical psychology and were avid readers of his work. We had also kept up, as much as we could, with the rapidly multiplying library of work by his students and colleagues, so we particularly appreciated the opportunities presented in these seminars. Leaving our three teenagers happily keeping house, with the backup of a neighbor if needed, we flew to our first Carl Jung seminar in Jung's home town of Küsnacht, Switzerland.

Küsnacht is some twenty minutes by train from Zurich, but a long distance, in both miles and access, from our home in Kansas City. Several of us often walked through the small town between classes, and it was then, in 1978, that the Jung family home, at Seestrasse #228, was pointed out to us. It sat only a mile or so from the Jung Institute.

Sometimes, walking by myself between classes, I liked to stop and stand on the sidewalk along this quiet street and gaze up the well-tended walkway to the stately house, rather like a gawking tourist. Truthfully, that was almost exactly what I was, just one of the crowds of people who find their way to Küsnacht each year in search of all they can gather and absorb of Jung's essence, which seems to hover, somehow, along the immaculate Swiss lanes and hedges of the town.

I wondered, standing on the sidewalk in front of the Jung family home as long as I dared, what I would say if someone came to the door and asked me just what I was doing there, staring at the house. I'd hastily explain I was in town attending a seminar at the Jung Institute and just wanted to see where the family had lived all those years. Then, embarrassed by my own fantasy of confrontation, I would quickly take my leave. But I often thought of that house and even briefly fantasized access, someday, somehow.

•

Ten years later, with our youngsters settled in other parts of the country, I was able to attend a full three-month semester of classes at the Jung Institute while Warren tended our home and his practice in Kansas City. This was a very special gift Warren had planned for me as a reward for completing my exams as a Licensed Clinical Social Worker—at the tender age of fifty—and leaving my career as a teacher and school administrator to join Warren's staff of eight therapists the following fall.

I flew to Switzerland.

On the first day of the three-month semester, I attended a welcome reception for new students and met Mr. Elton Josey, student representative of the Institute Curratorium. He greeted me cordially. We visited a bit, and he invited me to call him Elton. I asked if there might be a possibility of visiting the Jung family home that I'd only seen from the sidewalk on my first visit. Elton thought for a moment, then suggested I write to Franz Jung, Carl Jung's only son, who now occupied a part of the big house, and ask him. Elton added that Herr Jung felt a strong sense of family history and tried to accommodate requests of this nature when he could. I knew his father, Carl Jung, had been deceased for some twenty-seven years by then, but I did not know Herr Franz occupied the family home.

As the reception came to a close, a young woman approached me and introduced herself as Joan Smith of California. She had overheard my question to Elton and asked if I would be willing to include her in any request I might make to Herr Franz Jung to visit the family home. We chatted for a bit, and I agreed to her request, but I also told her I was not at all sure I would have the courage to write to him.

In retrospect, I'm convinced that if it had not been for Joan's urging, I might have missed the entire experience! But as it was, I agreed to keep her posted if I found myself brave enough to undertake the writing task. That evening, I did, indeed, draft a letter to Herr Jung, but it far from suited me. I did some self-examination. Why, exactly, was making a simple request to Herr Franz Jung such an impossible task? Surely he could say no if he wished. Soon I realized it was difficult because I feared being thought of as rude or idly curious. Old war-time stories of "ugly Americans" who were insensitive to the very private nature of Europeans crossed my mind. Yet I knew I was neither crude nor insensitive, and my desire to visit the Seestrasse house was very powerful, rising from deep within me.

The "ugly American" stories, I suddenly realized, came directly from my own history. As a young woman in my late teens, I lived in Stuttgart, Germany, with my parents as an army dependent. World War II had barely ended little more than a year previously when we moved there in October of 1946 to join my father, a United States Army officer, whose job it was to develop and supervise the U.S. Army Postal Service for peace time. My mother had lectured me endlessly about careful manners and how important it was for me to be considerate and as inconspicuous as possible among the German civilians, who were still enduring great suffering. Many still had scarce food or heat for cold houses, and poor shoes. Actually, what my mother feared was not so much that I would be rude, but that at age seventeen, I would be noticed by my warm clothes and lively spirit and possibly be vulnerable to some sort of unexpected encounter I wouldn't know how to handle.

Once I realized what was keeping me from writing to Herr Jung—the risk of being thought of as rude—I at least got the why of my hesitancy straightened out.

The following Sunday morning, I walked to the Hotel Sonne for breakfast since my own hotel closed its kitchens on Sundays, and I unexpectedly met Joan enjoying *kline frushtick*, a small breakfast. We sat together and became better acquainted. She was a musicologist who taught in the graduate school of the University of Southern California, an Arnold Schoenberg scholar, and a violinist. She was, as was I, auditing the spring/summer seminars at the Jung Institute and hoping to visit friends in the music world in Vienna later in the summer.

We talked amiably of our mutual interests, and as I prepared to leave, she asked if I had as yet written to Franz Jung. I confessed my first letter had left me unsatisfied, and I was still wrestling with it on some level. "I understand," she said. "It does seem like an imposition, doesn't it? Well, if you do write to him, let me know."

I drafted a second letter to Herr Jung, but my words seemed laced with an apologetic tone that made me uncomfortable, and with which I had not yet come to terms. So I put it aside, feeling that same fluster of embarrassment my fantasy on the Seestrasse sidewalk had produced.

That night, I dreamed of my oldest son's friend Scott Malcolmson, who had become an international journalist. In the dream, Scott visited me, or I him. He appeared to be in his office, or at least what seemed to be his office, complete with a typewriter on his desk. He seemed not his own actual age—some twenty-three years—but more as a thoroughly competent and self-assured adult, yet still unmistakably Scott. He regarded me in a challenging pose. No words were exchanged, but I felt confronted, as if he had accusingly said, "Well?"

In the morning, I knew I needed some of Scott's spirit, his belief in his right to follow his own sense of story. Or perhaps what I needed was some of his young-man energy! I later recognized this as a remnant of my own constant ventures back into my journalism skills of by-gone years and the omnipresent, yet barely resistible strong sense that permeates my family of writers.

In the second week of May, I finally dropped a brief, straightforward request at the local post office addressed to Herr Franz Jung, asking if I and a friend might visit him, and if there was a possibility of visiting his father's famous retreat, the Tower at Böllingen.

To my surprise and pleasure, within four days I received a cordial answer, inviting me to telephone and set a time for the three of us to have tea. I called, and we set a date for May 24 at 5:00 P.M.

I saved the letter, long-stored in the famous "monster in the closet" suitcase, and reproduce it here:

Dear Mrs. Molton,

In answer to your fine letter of May 5, I tell you that you are welcome to see me at Seestr228, whenever you want.

Actually, we should make some kind of agreement to meet. So please call me up when you have time for a cup of tea one of these next days, Friday, Monday, Tuesday, then after May 28–June 13, I am gone for holidays.

To visit Böllingen in summer times is probably not to do. It is out of my possibilities because that place is run by our own Management. During the whole summer, the house is rented to some branches of the many relatives of Jung heirs.

The intention is to have at Böllingen our open house in late October or November for graduating scholars from the Jung Institute. Before then, I have no rights to send visitors there or to *go to Böllingen with friends. For your friends who have to go to the states in early July, the only chance would be to go at their own risk and knock at the door.*

Sometimes a charitable soul opens, sometimes not.

Sincerely yours, F. Jung

(But please don't tell them I sent you!)

I was, of course, delighted. The note carried both the charm of a person not entirely comfortable writing in English and the cordiality of a genuine invitation. His voice on the phone was equally friendly, and we set the date for the 24th of May at 5:00 P.M.

On that day, Joan and I walked to the Blumet Balzer Garteneri to pick out a suitable flower gift for our host. We selected a potted Gerber daisy with two deep orange blossoms, and the clerk wrapped them for us. Orange—my color for courage.

We headed for Seestrasse at about 4:45 P.M., walking slowly in the afternoon sunlight, wanting to make sure we arrived at exactly the appointed time. Both of us admitted to being a bit nervous.

At exactly 5:00 P.M., we turned onto the path leading to the house and noticed the well-kept grounds. Joan said, "Herr Jung is almost eighty. He must have some help tending such a large garden and grounds area!" On our right, vegetable and flower beds ranged among grassy slopes and towering trees, and to the left, a plowed area under some sort of screen with unidentifiable spring plantings. A small car and a woman's bicycle sat untended in the driveway. A red Citroen was parked in a sort of lean-to garage, somewhat disguised by trees and heavy foliage.

Having made hasty notes from my reading, I recalled that Dr. Carl Jung and his family had moved here when the house was new in the spring of 1909, shortly after the birth of baby Franz in November of 1908. The big, new house was designed by and built for Dr. Jung, his wife, two daughters, and the infant son, Franz. Prior to this time, they had lived among the faculty resident staff members at the Burgholzli Mental Hospital.

Joan and I noticed the famous Latin inscription over the door, VOCATUS ATQUE NON VOCATUS DEUS ADERIT, which I later learned to translate: "Called or not called, God is present," written by Erasmus in the 1500s, regarding the ancient words of the Oracle at Delphi.

Through my research and questioning the staff at the Institute, I had learned Franz and his wife, Lilly, resumed residence at the family home in 1966, five years after his father's death in 1961. He now owned the property at the renowned address. I can only surmise that something called him to assume the role of resident host in this famous and fine old house as a sort of curator and arbiter of the family archives. Virtually hundreds of guests have visited him here, at his invitation, to meet with him in his father's library and talk with him about his father, family history, and the vast area of scholarship Carl Jung's work had generated.

A brass bell placket hung on each side of the door. The one on the left bore the engraving F. Jung: Architect, and we selected that one to ring.

Joan suddenly remembered how, in Switzerland, it is polite to remove the wrapping paper before presenting flowers, and we did so hastily, stuffing the wrapping in my leather tote bag just as Herr Jung opened the door.

He was a tall, imposing man who resembled his father's pictures. His strength and bearing was that of a man in his late sixties rather than one of seventy-nine years. He was erect, vital, buoyantly energetic, and dressed in tan slacks with a louden-green jacket over a gray shirt and with a dapper green-and-black silk ascot at his throat, European style. He greeted me cordially by name, and I introduced Joan. He said we should walk up the stairs, two flights, and not be worried if the family dog, Mackie, barked at us.

At his indication, I led the way. The wide stairs were covered with handsome oriental carpeting and each stair braced with fine brass fittings. Somewhere along the walls of the stairway, I recall a painting of a white horse, but perhaps I noticed it when we were leaving. It made a firm impression on my memory since I had been studying animals as symbolic images at the time.

On the first landing, I paused a moment, letting some of my thoughts surface briefly. The stairway was wide and bright, flooded with light, comfortable, but quiet. Herr Jung waved us up another flight with a cordial good humor. On the left as we entered his apartment was a doorway leading to a kitchen area. He stopped to get a saucer to put under the Gerber daisy and moved to place it in the hallway. I mentioned to him that the blooms were the same color as the bright orange-and-white kitchen I could see from the doorway, and he laughed. "Yes," he said, "I should put them in the kitchen by the window," and he placed the flowering plant in a pool of afternoon sunlight on the kitchen table. I offered to help him prepare the tea tray, but he waved us ahead. Joan and I went into the main room of this floor, passing a room on our right that I later learned had been his father's consultation room.

The main room we entered was Carl Jung's world-famous library. We were greeted by Mackie, the aged and friendly family dog, who entered the room from the open glass doors leading to a balcony overlooking the gardens and facing the lake. Mackie did a good bit of ceremonial singing, wagging, and welcoming, and soon our host joined us with a large tea tray.

My own sensate function, summoned to attention by the uniqueness of the occasion, helps me recall, even these many years later, the teapot handle fitted with a cheerful white potholder covered in red hearts and a fragrant apple pastry, *apfelkuchen*, the making of which I later discovered was a creative domestic talent and skill of Herr Jung's and which he regularly prepared for his guests.

Soon we were all seated, Joan and I on the couch along the north wall and Herr Jung in a chair with his back to the open balcony doors.

I immediately inquired about his health, as on the phone, he'd mentioned a trip to his physician that day. He said he suffered from a pain in his left shoulder, a calcification problem that now and then kept him awake at night, and he would take some physical therapy before leaving on May 28 for his holidays in Salonica. I mentioned that my friend Joan was a violinist and also suffering a temporary handicap of tendinitis of the wrist, and they began to discuss various hot and cold treatments. Herr Jung said how distressing this must be for her since "to play the violin is of the soul and gives pleasure to so many people." His relaxed use of the word "soul" signaled for me that our conversation would be comfortable and free.

Our host smiled and went on to tell us his son Andreas and family lived on the lower level of the house. His wife's name was Verena, and they had two children, Michael and Sophie. Michael, Herr Franz's grandson, used to play the violin but had taken to playing the piano. Since he was not taking instructions, he was apt to play a bit loud, but altogether the arrangement of having two families living in the house was very satisfactory since he could keep an eye on the grandchildren when their parents went off to the theater, and he could go out evenings without being concerned about burglary.

We returned to the subject of music. Herr Jung did not play an instrument but was particularly fond of baroque music. He said that when attending concerts, his friends liked to sit where they could see the musicians, but he preferred closing his eyes to enjoy the emotional experience of the music. He was often moved to tears, he said.

A conversation ensued regarding a musician who had recently visited him, a Mr. T., whose world seemed fraught with a vagueness of symbol and metaphor beyond Herr Jung's understanding. He went on to say that his father preferred to work with those who had at least one foot in reality, and he was not sure this musician and his father would have been able to work together. He mentioned his father had no musical background and probably would have been at a loss to understand Mr. T.'s theory that some musical constructs were comparable to various alchemical notations. Herr Jung added that he, himself, found his father's alchemical work a bit difficult to understand. Joan and I exchanged smiles and agreed we found it so, as well. Franz said his father had no knowledge of music and might not have been able to discuss a premise regarding alchemical notation similarities, and added the legendary story of those who asked his father if he believed in God, to which his father replied, "No. I do not believe. I know."

Following that familiar line of thought, Franz said his father had been very interested in people who had some sort of personal experience in transcendence and not so much those who merely accepted this as dogma. He added that at the time of his father's death, he actually received a letter from someone in California, inquiring if the family had retained some cells of their father in ice cryonics so that he could be restored at the time of judgment! I wondered at the time if this contact were from the enthusiastic cytogenetic people in California whom, I had read, were particularly interested in dead geniuses. Franz shook his head and shrugged, implying such an inquiry reflected dogma gone somewhat awry.

I do not recall how the conversation turned at this juncture to his childhood experiences with his father. Perhaps we first talked about the room itself, which had been his father's library, and for a period of time, his study as well. Franz recalled that his father had found all the activity and sparkle of the lake outside the window distracting and preferred to study in the smaller, more secluded consultation room next door. Sometimes the larger library was off limits to Franz as a child and sometimes not. He gestured, holding his hands about eighteen inches apart and reminded us he had come to this house when he was only three months old, in 1909, as the third child and only son. After him, two younger sisters were born, filling out the family count to five females and two males. He said, "My father did not have much to do with me until I could both walk and swim. Then I became his companion." He told us of an early recollection as a boy of about five years old, lying in the bottom of a wooden boat while his father rowed from a standing position, towering against the sky.

"That was," he said, "a very vivid picture and created a feeling of absolute trust."

He went on to say that from that time on, Franz was often in his father's company, particularly on Saturdays and Sundays, while his sisters remained more with their mother at home.

Franz and his father ventured outside on weekends together. "First to the Tobel where there was water and wonderful clay, and we would build little houses and rivers and come home all muddy!" His hands gestured his mother's aghast greetings when they arrived home.

Later, he and his father spent a lot of time in the garden house at the south end of the lake, making mosaics of stones and sand. Part of Franz's participation was to collect stones of assorted shapes and colors and take them to his father to use in his designs. Soon they were working on building little sand houses. Before long, they worked out a manner to develop their houses with better sturdiness. His father thought they could make small bricks out of mortar for their constructions and found a castoff baking tray belonging to his wife, Emma. Soon they were cutting the warm mortar into miniature bricks for their small houses. He said, "We developed the idea that the walls must be two layers thick, with sand between, and reeds used for ceilings and roofs."

The first year of this game, Franz was the sole helper, although sometimes Emma and the girls would come down to the beach to watch and talk. "Like a group of women knitting and talking for relaxation," he said. Later, a relative of Emma who was also an architect joined the project. It was a pleasant family pastime, he told us. As he so thoroughly described this operation and the specificity of the plans, I began to wonder if perhaps this was the beginning of Franz's later career as an architect.

Soon they became very skillful and were dismayed when the tide would come and demolish their creations. "Finally," he said, "we put into practice moving the sturdy little houses out to the sea wall where they were safe from the tides." Together, they constructed a harbor town with a church, a school, and over time, as many as thirty houses.

He continued, "Of course, some of this game also went on up at Böllingen," after his father purchased the property and made plans for building when Franz was fourteen years old.

Franz went on to explain the situation regarding visiting the Böllingen Tower retreat, about which I had inquired in my first letter to him. He said that various family members now request time to stay there during the summer months. He said the requests were made to the family central managing board of five members, one member from each of the five families. Normal periods of residence were from April to October since there was neither central heat nor electricity, and water only available through the pump at the sink.

He went on to say the primitive nature of Böllingen was an important part of being there, and members of the family agreed it should be kept exactly as his father intended, even in its primitive state.

"But," Franz continued, "there is nothing much to see: old moss, dirt, stones. You could go into the hills and see the same thing."

Knowing his father's fame, I thought, "Well, maybe, but not quite . . ."

To our delight, Franz turned to further childhood memories:

My father had a great respect for me as his son and would allow me to do anything I wished. But he said I must take responsibility for what I did. Once, when the lake was very low and there were hundreds of dried reeds around the rim of the water, I had the idea that I could start a fire and burn the reeds, which would be quite the thing to see, a ring of fire around the lake! I discussed this with my father who agreed that this would indeed be a great thing to see, all the reeds burn up! "Yes, yes," he said. *And then added, almost too softly for me to hear, "and then, if along with the bright fire that would be so interesting to see, the boathouse should burn also with the reeds . . . Ah, yes. What then?" In that moment, I knew I would be responsible if the boathouse burned up!*

He went on to tell another childhood story of a time when his father and some of the children were housebound with whooping cough and confined to one large room of the house. His father was the leader, and they played many games of his invention. At one point, they played a game requiring buying and selling. His father painted large stacks of currency since a great deal of money was required to play the game. Franz particularly remembered his father's painstaking drawing of the play currency and the care he took to make the bills seem real. "He very much liked to draw and paint in this manner and seemed to find this refreshing," he said.

Herr Jung went to the bookshelves and brought back two books to show us. The first was Carl Jung's personal hand-illustrated copy of *Septem Sermones Ad Mortuous* (Seven Sermons to the Dead) lettered in beautiful Gothic script, and handed it to me. The first letters of each paragraph were ornately painted in reds and blues with touches of gold tempera, and the script in black. The paper was a heavy weight and light brownish in color.

I held the book, my hands trembling, feeling suddenly overwhelmed with what I was holding, and recalled what I knew of his father's life history. Only a few copies of this book had been printed and not generally circulated. As I leafed through, I saw the book also contained Carl Jung's account of some of his dreams from 1917. At the top of several of the dream pages, he had made intricate paintings of coins. Some dreams had one coin, some two, one three, a few no coins at all. Each coin was painted yellow with what looked like tempera paint and allowed to dry, then etched with what appeared to be brown detail added in his careful, painstaking manner. I asked Franz if he knew what the coins represented.

He took the manuscript from my hands, studied it carefully, and shook his head. "No, I do not know what they represent, only that my father was very fond of painting in this manner."

It was clear each small coin painting had taken a good bit of time. As I studied the dreams, I began to think it was rather as if the act of painting the coins might have been done as a way of remaining within each dream while considering the content on a deeper level, rather like what we would call doodling while pondering something else.

When I mentioned this to Franz, he mused, shook his head, and shrugged, as if to say, *who knows?*

The second book Franz brought to the table was a copy of the same book from the first professional printing, which his father had published in a limited edition for friends. Franz pointed out that the anagram on the printed edition appeared at the back instead of the front as it is in the original handwritten manuscript.

ANIGRAMA:
NAHTRIHCCUNDE
GAHINNEVERAHTUNIN
ZEHGESSURKLACH
ZUNUS

Franz talked about the mystery of the famous anagram, which had intrigued and baffled scholars over the years. He said, "At one time, a group of enthusiastic ones invited the family to a special occasion to announce the meaning of the anagram, which they had, after a great deal of work, translated." But at the announcement, Franz and other members of the family felt the conclusion reached by the scholars must be inaccurate or some sort of pontification since the words were not at all consistent with their father as they knew him, and were, in fact, meaningless to them.

He said it was Frau Anielia Jaffe who later studied the anagram, out of her excellent intuition and knowledge of his father. Her translation revealed words that were unspectacular and pertained to an indication of where and when the manuscript was written, which might explain the shift of position from the front of the hand-written manuscript to the back of the printed version.

Later, as I thought more about this, I wondered if Carl Jung might have done the anagram rather as he had carefully painted the coins at the head of the pages of dreams. It is only my fantasy that he might have attended to the anagram as a small mind game, enjoying the look of the fine letters on the page, while he worked at a deeper level of consciousness to ponder the meaning of the work itself since the letters of each word were so carefully and beautifully painted, or silently articulated.

At a later date, when I mentioned this again to Franz, he mused and shook his head once again, perplexed.

But that first afternoon, our discussion of the *Septem Sermones Ad Mortuous* manuscript continued as we recalled together that Jung, later on, had not wanted this manuscript included in the collected works and only agreed to its inclusion in an appendix of *Memories, Dreams, Reflections* as an historical footnote. Franz thought this might have been because his father had presented the work as written by Basilides in Alexandria, a legendary second-century Gnostic folk figure, and his father might have thought he could be "accused of plagiarism!" This said with a laugh and the matter was dropped as we moved on to other topics.

Here, I stop to recall how I remember the details of this room. The library was not large, perhaps twelve by sixteen feet. The walls were lined with Jung's books, and the ribs of the bookcases carried alphabetical listings marked with hand-lettered symbols starting with Aa, Ab, Ac, etcetera. These shelves continued above and below the windows on that wall and above the glass doors leading to the small balcony, overlooking the lake. The room drew its character from the lake, in full view, and all was very light and comfortable. We sat facing a wall where there was a recessed area among the bookcases with a shelf and mirror, and on the shelf sat a large and stunning Grecian urn. All the woodwork was painted a soft gray-green.

In the southeast corner of the room stood a large desk-table. Behind it, a wooden chair. I recall I had, at one time, seen a photograph somewhere of Carl Jung, seated there and studying in his library. The upholstered chairs were of a gray-blue cast, and two Queen Anne chairs were covered with maroon brocade. Oriental carpets covered the wood flooring, and a low serving table stood in front of the couch upon which Franz had placed his prepared treat. The west wall held a magnificent view of the gardens and Lake Zurich beyond, and at the opposite wall was a large and omnipresent tile stove familiar in older Swiss homes.

Franz told us he had lived in this house all during his boyhood until he went off to school in Stuttgart. He later established his architectural firm, married Lilly, and raised four sons, all the while living in Küsnacht. His father died in 1961, and Franz returned to live in the family home with Lilly, where she died in 1983.

His architectural firm's office, which Franz designed, was now managed by his son Christof, who lived with his family in the house where Franz and Lilly raised their sons, a typical Franz Jung house, one side wood, three sides mortar, at Obere Heslibachstrasse #79 in Küsnacht. The home also served as the family's architectural firm. Two of his sons are architects, Christof and Andreas; Peter is a psychiatrist; and Lorenz is a psychotherapist.

While Franz spoke of his father's work with pleasure and pride, he was careful to tell us that he, himself, was in no way a psychologist. Later, I discovered he had made a serious study of his father's work after his father died, but he had never submitted himself to Jungian analysis.

We carried the tea things and remaining crumbs from the fine *apfelkuchen* out to the kitchen after more than two hours of this interesting exchange. Franz then led us to Dr. Carl Jung's consultation room, adjoining the library, where he saw patients. Franz told us it had been changed some although it remained still as a comfortable study. This was the room Dr. Jung loved, where he could have total privacy and remain undistracted by the lake and its traffic.

For consultations, he sat at a desk while the patient would talk to him from a comfortable chair, set at a diagonal. Franz pointed out three mullioned windows, the top third of which were beautiful stained-glass replicas of windows in a thirteenth-century church in Konigsfelden, near Baden, sixty kilometers away. The left section held a scene depicting Lazarus, the right one a flagellation, and the center panel a cruciform.

The room had a beautiful soft light, reflected from the brilliant panels. Franz said his grandchildren loved to come upstairs and play in this room, and I saw a scattering of children's toys in one corner. I thought any child would love to play here as the room is so conducive to accessing the imaginative world of children. Everything was contained, quiet, warm, and welcoming.

We returned to the library for a moment on the way out. I paused by the Grecian vase and said something about how it must be a family treasure. Franz asked how I knew it was a family treasure. I was a bit startled by the abruptness of his question and answered carefully that if it were in my house, it would be a family treasure.

Franz seemed almost relieved that I'd given him an invitation to talk about the vase. "It was one of the great mysteries of my return here. I found it in pieces in the attic, and no one seemed to know anything about it," he said. "I took the shards to a professional artisan to have it restored and appraised. As I suspected, it was authentic, dating from about 350 B.C.!"

He still sounded surprised at his discovery and showed us where it had been carefully mended and where it had been repaired previously after an earlier breakage. No one knew where it came from or how it had come to lie in pieces in the attic. A great deal of conjecture arose about it among family members. One of his sisters found a line in one of Carl Jung's published letters to Freud, which read, "My beautiful vase (*krug*) arrived safely," but no one knew for sure if this was the same vase, particularly since *krug* in German connotes a fairly ordinary object. The vase stood perhaps eighteen inches in height and ten inches wide. The full tale of the Greek vase may never be known.

"There is always," Franz said, "a conjecture."

Franz took us out on the balcony for a last look at the gardens and lake. He said, "Lilly used to enjoy sitting here during the final days of her illness, watching the water and the birds."

We saw the south end of the property, the boathouse, and the sea wall where the small village had been set. I noticed the trees: a great elm, the plane tree, and poplars that cast the shadows of early evening across the flagstone paths. The three of us stood quietly for a moment in the twilight, aware that we had shared a stretch of time reaching far back in history, and yet ahead, somehow, into all our lives. I sensed, for a flashing moment, the hours I'd spent here would make a difference, a change, somehow, in my own life.

At the front door, we thanked our host for his kindness and wished him a pleasant journey to Salonica. He replied it was an interesting place for him to visit because, as yet, the island had not been combed over too much by tourists and archaeologists, and relics were still to be found by scraping the sand with one's foot. He gestured, whisking the floor with the toe of one shoe. He also said he very much liked inviting people to the house who asked to come, but it was not comfortable for him if too many came at once.

Joan and I walked down the path in silence for a while. "A little like Salonica..." she said, and I took her to mean we would turn up our own story about this visit. We walked a mile up the hill to have a look at Obere Heslibachstrasse #79, the typical Franz Jung house, which in this case carried the full history of Franz's family life.

•

I kept a copy of my letter to him, written some weeks later while preparing to leave Küsnacht. The delay was an acknowledgment that Franz was on vacation in Salonica and would not, perhaps, see my letter until later.

Dear Mr. Jung,   *June 18, 1988*

Alas, I have been unable to secure a machine, so I shall do my best to write in a legible hand, and ask your forbearance. I can hardly express to you how much I enjoyed the opportunity to meet you and how fortunate I feel to have had that pleasure. It was an experience of enormous interest for me, of being in the surroundings in which you were raised, and about which you shared some memories of your father, mother, and boyhood. When I arrived back in my room after our visit, I sat down at my desk and wrote everything I could recall, starting with my sitting in your father's famous library, and also all I could recall of my time with you. To my surprise, I found I have many pages of notes.

There are, however, three recollections, particularly, which I must share with you. One was the experience of holding your father's manuscript of Septem Sermones ad Mortuous in my hands. When I returned to my room, I read his account of writing that manuscript in his autobiography, Memories, Dreams, Reflections, and especially the part where he wrote, "It began with a restlessness..." and relates how part of the restlessness affected you as a nine-year-old with an anxiety dream about which you drew a picture the next day. I wondered if your picture is still among the family archives, the one called The Picture of the Fisherman. It must have been, indeed, an extraordinary picture for a child of nine.

I have also thought of the pictures of coins your father painted in that book and the dreams he recorded. As I recall, some pages had one coin, some two, and I believe, at least one page had three. It occurred to me that perhaps this was your father's way of estimating the value, or importance, of each dream, or his own understanding of it. Or perhaps it was an entirely different sort of reasoning. But it remains in my mind, and I am apt to ask myself of my own dreams: "Now, is this a one, two, or three-coin dream?" In other words, the coins could represent some sort of value, or significance, or current message of importance to a dreamer from the unconscious, or perhaps, even what remains still to be discovered, or is not yet understood.

My third powerful recollection of my visit with you is the story you told of lying in a boat as a child, age five years, and seeing your father rowing above you, towering over you against the sky. In some ways, this experience of yours could be a metaphor for so many of us who have taken the journey into the waters of the unconscious, trusting your father's word. I, too, sensed something of his strength and his power.

I keep a picture of your father on a credenza in the office where I see my clients. From time to time, someone points to the picture and asks if that man is my father. Now I will be able to say, "No, he is not my real father, but I have met his real son." And once again the story of my visit with you will be told. It was also a pleasure for me to walk with Joan to see Obere Heslibachstrasse #79, a "typical Franz Jung house," as is said. It has a fine character, a gracious quality, and is at ease on the land, like the gentleman who designed it.

Yours sincerely, Mary Dian Molton

Franz replied to my letter with enthusiasm and thus began our singular friendship.

Dear Mrs. Molton,   July 7, 1988

I thank you for your very nice letter of June 18, which touched me enormously. I realize that sometimes and for some people, being at Seestr in my father's house is more than just a kind of routine sight-seeing. You really could express your impressions and your feelings so well that I am very grateful of your incentive to write. I do not normally get such good letters, thanking for a visit!

Whatever I can do sometime for you, please let me know! You mentioned in your letter that my father was writing about me in

Memories, Dreams, Reflections. I had nearly forgotten about it, and I immediately took that book from the shelf to read it again. It was nearly as if I had never heard it before!

It is unhappy that my drawing of the fisherman is long ago missing and probably lost in my boyhood.

As I mentioned to you in my earlier answer about Böllingen, it will be an occasion to visit the tower in late October with the group of diploma candidates. Normally, Frau Weber from the Institute gives me the list of about fifteen to sixteen people who are finishing their studies. I'm having "open house" on a Saturday toward the end of October. If ever you are here, please do not hesitate to contact me in September or October.

Wishing you all the good, I am,

Sincerely, Franz Jung

Following this exchange and prior to any mention of a possible further extension of this friendship, I put my thoughts into notes about Franz:

While hundreds of guests have visited, at his invitation, to meet him in C. G.'s library and talk with him about his father, his family history, and the vast areas of scholarship and conjecture that his father's work has generated, he carries this task with an impressive grace. One senses, in his presence, a commitment to this singular, very specific mode of hospitality that respects the history and tradition of his family and indeed something also of the spiritual essence of his father and his place of true genius in the world order.

But in no way is Franz a mere tour guide of his father's intimate surroundings. He is, also, a man who manages to be quite himself, comfortable in that selfhood, and cordially apart from the world of psychological inquiry, while still maintaining a healthy respect for his father's work. He also carries a lively interest in the people who associate themselves with the Jungian world.

Something of his own pose in this effort seems to me to be a rather remarkable achievement of selfhood. He seems both comfortable with what he knows of his father's story and also quite free of it, a man involved, yet certainly quite comfortably and intentionally apart.

I can feel, or hope that I have, somehow, not seen the last of him.

CHAPTER TWO

Mutual Interests

❋

SEVERAL MONTHS FOLLOWED DURING WHICH FRANZ AND I exchanged correspondence. We agreed we would meet again during another seminar in January 1989 at the Jung Institute. It was to be a series of instructions on the use of psychodrama and dreams. I had been deeply involved studying and training in psychodrama in the States, and in addition, there were plans for me to develop a psychodrama program for in-patients at two local psychiatric hospitals in the fall. I was very pleased there was sufficient interest in this skill at the Jung Institute in Switzerland.

During the previous spring, I'd had the pleasure of preparing an evening event for an organization of play readers, timed for Midsummer Night. I designed and directed a production of play-reading the Fool's scenes from Shakespeare's *A Midsummer Night's Dream*. The scenes were performed in a beautiful rustic garden in Kansas City and made a lovely evening of Reader's Theatre, produced with not too much work and enjoyed by all who participated and attended. My interest in psychodrama no doubt arose in part from my interest and participation in theatre.

A few words regarding psychodrama might be useful. Let's suppose you brought me a dream, and this dream is about your little sister. The two of us would act out the dream and see what arose from that. In a large group, we would then tell the dream and choose characters in the room to play the roles. Say a person brought a dream of a mother and an aunt and a child in a car accident. The group would dramatize the dream, giving the leader more material to help the dreamer understand it. Helping the dreamer be outside the dream, so to speak, helps them see it from another perspective than fear.

I once had a prophetic dream about Böllingen. I was a little girl walking through the gate with a group of people and was so excited. I had that dream before I even met Franz. There were adults and me, the little girl, running around.

After completing a master's degree in clinical social work, which entitled me to be a licensed colleague, I was starting my own practice. I had also been involved in my own personal Jungian analysis work, first in Denver with Diplomate Jungian analyst Clarissa Pinkola Estés. During that period, Warren and I undertook a "commuter marriage" while I began my analysis. Meanwhile, he was holding down the home front in Kansas City with his practice, while I worked for the Denver Public Broadcasting Company, managing the educational TV programming for twenty-three states and helping develop materials for several schools and colleges via the new satellite delivery systems. We were able to see each other only a few times a month. The work was exciting, and I got a good start on analysis, but we were glad to terminate that period. After returning home to Kansas City, I continued with Jungian analysis and analytical studies under the tutelage of Diplomate Jungian analyst Gary Hartman, with whom, over the following several years, I continued analysis and analytical studies. I felt it important to learn how members of the Jungian community in Switzerland were combining psychodrama with Jung's dream work. Toward the end of December, I wrote to Franz, telling him I hoped he would have a wonderful Christmas holiday. He responded soon after.

Dear Mrs. Molton,   *January 3, 1989*

Thank you for your letter. Christmas was full with invitations, good food, etc., so I am glad it is over now, only my table is full of letters that have to be answered. As I became eighty a month ago, I have also presents and letters to thank for that jubilee!

Between Christmas and New Year, I had a book, The Gnostic Jung, by Stephen Hoeller sent to me on your initiative. I had heard of it earlier, but never seen. Now I am very interested to read it. Now I've only read the prologue, which is most promising. I did not know you are acquainted with Mr. Hoeller, and now I understand better the passage in your M.S. when I gave you the original writing of that dream in Seven Sermons to the Dead by C. G.

I just sent a card to Stephen Hoeller to thank him, and my thanks are also for you because of your generosity. I think I have still somewhere in my home original prints from 1916, and I will send one to Mr. Hoeller. He might be pleased to have it.

I hope to see you very soon. For the meantime, I am yours,

Sincerely, F. Jung

I was also particularly interested in talking further with Franz about the possibility of my working on another monograph concerning his involvement in his deceased father's world, with the notion of publication of some sort in my mind. He had not responded, as yet, on this subject. But also, neither had he as yet declined, although I knew he was aware of my interest.

I sent him my set of notes on our first visit. Along with his kind additions and corrections, we had also begun an exchange concerning his interest in America's pre-history, particularly the Paleolithic era at the time of the Complex Folsom, the Paleo-Indian archaeological culture of North America and their excavations at the rim of the Cimarron River, a tributary of the Red River in northeastern New Mexico. Franz had told me at some time that he had decided, years ago, not to visit America, although once he had hoped he might be able to do so. When I wrote and asked his reason, he told me in one of our telephone conversations, "Well, when one speaks of 'America' I just do not know what they are talking about. So many different climates at the same time! Too many different landscapes, deserts, dialects, oceans, mountains! But when one speaks of Switzerland, everyone knows exactly what they mean. It is mostly snow, skiing, ice! But when one speaks of America, it is just too big!" This was said with some emphasis. And so, he had made his decision not to venture a trip.

I had never encountered this sort of reasoning, but I soon realized that at his age and with what little I knew of the geographic realities of the size of most countries in Europe, he had made an understandable point. With such wide differences in climate and geography in such a large space, the U.S.A. is difficult to comprehend comfortably, especially when compared to tidy and contained Switzerland.

About this time, I found a yellow sheet of paper with notes I'd made after an early conversation with Franz.

C. G. Jung plunged into the unconscious and drew from it the inner forms of the archetypes. Franz grew up watching and perhaps even unknowingly helping his father fashion outward manifestations of his inner restless quests in stone, mosaic mandalas, and small houses built with cubes of mortar, sand, reeds, and stone—outward structures that might have given sturdy form to his father's inner world. Franz somehow grasped, as he grew older, that his own world had to be architecture. It perhaps stretches the metaphoric consonance, but there feels to be some sort of tangible and inherent creative plunges that were similar.

When I first visited Franz Jung at the Seestrasse home, delighted to have the opportunity to hear him speak of his father, mother, and sisters, delighted to sit in the fine old library and listen, share, feel as if somehow Franz was a manifestation of C. G.; there in his likeness in his son, and it was easy to slip into that miasma. But as my time with Franz developed, I began to see him as totally himself, a separate man, and his own story took on for me a turn more vital and alive as Franz began to share with me what the design of houses meant to him. The houses are a rather remarkable achievement.

Perhaps one could search through the archives for tales of the children of the great and see how they fared, suffered, or otherwise transcended the numen or "divine mind" of their famous fathers or mothers; look for indications of wounds, grievances, pain and pride; and come up with a sort of generic complex endured by such people. Such accounts sit, doubtless, on the shelves of libraries of this century and past ones. Somehow, Franz seemed to have transcended any sort of generic categorization. He was himself, remarkably free. And this freedom, I believe, enabled him to be where he was, do what he did, and live in his father's story as a rather splendid example of what those of us who work in the Jungian didactic might wish our children could achieve and become.

What must it be like to be talented and able and been fathered by one of the world's great geniuses, one who had ventured beyond others of his time in his field of endeavor and gathered a sizeable portion of the world to his feet? Does the son, struggling with his own identity among the world of men, tend to erase himself as "'less than" to the genius of his father? Does he, then, enter his own professional life with a hindrance of overvaluing or undervaluing his own gifts? What seems to me to be so remarkable about Franz is his acceptance of himself as he is, a gifted architect of passion and accomplishment, a devoted husband and father to four sons, an amused and lively scholar of anthropology and archeology in the manner in which gentlemen pursue their interests in their later years, not as ambitious innovators but as heartily enjoyed pleasant pastimes, and as cordial and interested hosts to those who come to Father's door?

In order to reciprocate his kindness to me and because of his interest in pre-historic America, I wondered if there were something I could do or find that might further his historical interests regarding America, something that might be difficult for him to research from so far away, complicated by another language.

With the fortunate help of a family-related archaeologist, Mr. Jack Bertram, I learned of Dr. Dennis Stanford, the Smithsonian Institute's authority in this area of research. I contacted him by mail, and Dr. Stanford kindly helped me secure a good reading list, which I sent to Franz.

Dear Franz,   March 20, 1989

I received your lovely letter complete with pictures from Els this week and enjoyed both very much.

While it is a bit early to announce, I have a wellspring of information on the Folsom Complex. I am pleased to relate a few steps which I believe will lead us in the right direction.

I have an archaeologist in my family named Jack Bertram, from the University of New Mexico. He is a delightful man and has been married to my sister's daughter for thirteen years.

Sincerely, Mary Dian

Franz responded to my letter immediately.

Dear Mary Diane,   March 28, 1989

Many thanks for your kind letter and the documentation about Stone Age USA. I studied these lists, and I think they are much too specialized, the only book which would give me an oversight is "Peopling of the New World" by Ericson-Taylor-Bergen, and also this one is full of detailed tables which are not so easy for me to understand. Anyway, even if it is a thick book, I would be interested very much to go into it.

You are welcome with your telephone call on 20th January 7:00 P.M. In February 1989 I am at Küsnacht all through that month. It is only after the first week of March I hope to leave for a fortnight skiing at Engadin. Sorry for my shortness, I am in a bit of a hurry and want to post letter.

Franz

We also found a mutual interest in the subject of alchemy, which Franz had mentioned during my first visit along with Joan. A close friend of Warren's and mine, the Hungarian portrait painter Frank Szasz, having heard of my trip and meeting with Franz, told us of his boyhood friend and now reputable scholar, Dr. Stephen Hoeller, who had recently written a substantial book entitled *The Gnostic Jung*. Through Frank's suggestion and kindness, I was able to meet Dr. Hoeller and secure a copy of this book for Franz, who wrote that it had just arrived, and he had read the introduction and found it very promising.

Franz graciously reciprocated by sending Dr. Hoeller a copy of the earliest private publication of the first edition of his father's work, *Septem Sermones Ad Mortuous*. This private edition of Jung's work, intended for just a few friends of Dr. Jung, turned out to be an important and splendid gift to Stephen Hoeller, who was indeed delighted.

As our relationship developed, the scars of pain and suffering, as well as pleasure, of course, became more humanly apparent. Our relationship grew by mail.

With Warren's blessing, I proceeded to engage a spot on the roster for a psychodrama seminar at the Jung Institute taught by Dr. Helmut Baraz and his wife, Eleanor, who had previously studied psychodrama with Zerka Moreno, the originator of this highly interesting skill set, and with whom I had also worked during the past year in two four-week sessions here in the States on how this therapy could be incorporated skillfully into Jungian therapy practice.

Consequently, my second face-to-face visit with Franz Jung occurred on the late afternoon of Saturday, January 28, 1989, at the Seestrasse house, once again in the library.

CHAPTER THREE

WE MEET AGAIN

❋

OUR CONVERSATION BEGAN ONCE MORE OVER FRANZ'S FRAGRANT *apfelkuchen*. I talked about our heavy workloads and Warren's interest in writing and publishing his poetry, as well as Warren's and my own private Jungian analysis. He listened closely to the information about my husband's career, questioned me thoroughly about Warren's background, first as a clergyman, then as professor of pastoral psychology, and finally his doctorate in family therapy that led to his private practice. When I added that Warren recently wrote the eulogy and led the ceremony for his father's funeral, he commented, "What a wonderful spirit of duty! I could not have stood straight for my father, nor my sons." Franz was also pleased to know Warren had insisted that a full set of Jung's *Collected Works* be purchased for the seminar library where he was teaching. He then requested the titles of Warren's published books, which I agreed to supply. He also questioned me about my professional background as president/headmistress of a private school with 500 students and 50 faculty members. We went on to discuss the current re-direction of my career and my preparation to become a licensed practicing psychotherapist. I mentioned that both Warren and I looked forward to our retirement years and more time for creative writing, in which we each had a strong interest.

Franz spoke, hesitantly, of his concerns regarding issues of "transference" as he understood the term as used by his father. His point being, was I, perhaps, caught in a transference regarding him and his father? I reassured him, once again, and added that as a career architect, manager of the family home, and the senior family member and custodial host, he was responsible for ensuring guests were of distinct importance to the Jungian genre as the development of Jungian lore continued to grow. I believe this reassured him as to the nature of my interest in him and also helped him understand I was a happily married professional woman with a beloved family of my own. As my own practice developed, I was interested in learning from him how a son adapts to the knowledge that his father is a world-celebrated psychology scholar as well as learning about the dynamics of the father/son axis. And I knew these topics were of interest to others as well. He explained that these areas of interest made him shy, but he visibly relaxed some. Or so it seemed to me, as we had both become more comfortable.

We discussed briefly what he thought was missing for him in my early manuscript, which I had sent to him. He suggested some corrections and negated my appreciation for his particular place in it all. At one point, Franz noticed I was making brief notes and invited me to sit in the chair behind the desk. I recalled the photo taken of Dr. Jung seated in this same chair behind this desk. With some hesitation, or incredulity—I don't know which—I sat down. Franz drew up a chair opposite me. Somehow, I settled in.

According to my notes, I spent five hours in Jung's library at Seestrasse #228, this time hearing what Franz was willing to share with me. The day after this meeting, I wrote notes to my analyst, Gary Hartman in Kansas City about feeling completely stunned by sitting in what had been Carl Jung's chair. I am certain Gary never received them because they were still in my old suitcase when I dug it out from the closet, and in part, because of my own embarrassment. But at this point, it seems a good idea to include them because of the completely honest and intense emotional response I experienced from being placed in Jung's chair. It also gives me some pleasure to re-visit, now, at this time of my eighty-six years, my own excitement in my discoveries of Carl Jung's work.

These notes were swiftly written on a separate pad when Franz left the room to rummage in the kitchen cabinet.

On-sitting-at-Carl-Jung's-desk-in-his-own-chair-in-his-own-library-across-from-his-son-Franz-who is pouring out his heart-his eyes sometimes full-mopping his eyes and his brow: Why does my body feel so stiff on this chair? It drags on me. I can't settle. My wool skirt hangs on the edge of this chair. I am aghast that Franz has seated me here. How can I sit in Carl Jung's chair? Can I excuse myself? Run away? Is he, Franz, too tired to go on? No. He wants this talk. I address my struggling ego, overwhelmed. "Now see here, body, you ARE HERE so try to find the curves and slopes of this chair and settle in!" Across from me is Herr Jung, trying to tell me something. He wipes his eyes. I must gather into myself and let him be, so he can go on. Why is this chair so formidable? My legs hang over the right side of the chair, so I must pull them under the desk. I can hear my own silent voice, chastising me: "Now then, HEFT yourself into the center of the chair, and put your legs under the table!" They will only obey by an angle, slightly off to my right. How can I do this? So I do the best I can, and GLUE my ear to his voice. This feels like riding a little boat, maybe, being propelled by an unseen center figure paddling steadily without my help. Perhaps this is what it is like when fragile EGO is attacked and wants to shrink away and can't let go, and soul takes over and does the job, regardless. There is a flow. Something OTHER steers the boat . . .

When Franz returned, he brought with him his mother Emma's very old tray upon which he and his father had baked their mortar and cut small bricks. He began to talk, once again, about the small village he built with his father on the sea wall when he was a boy. Again, he explained that the walls must be two bricks thick for the houses of this village, and then, again, described the roofing, fashioned of reeds. They built houses, a church, a school, some thirty structures in all, he said, on the sea wall.

It was during this descriptive story that I again had a sense of the young architect in him, growing. Franz talked of what he considered "form" to be the union of material, the environment of place, and the design. Here was the man, Franz, speaking of what came to be his own great interest and profession in its earliest manifestation as if the construction of the little village on the sea wall were a sort of manifesto. He explained the process in detail, his hands describing the size of the small buildings and the care with which they were constructed. But even more significant than the unfolding story, I began to understand the importance to him of this tender memory of closeness between himself and his father from his early years. At the telling, he occasionally had tears in his eyes. I began to understand how, over the years, Böllingen came together in Franz's mind as an intimate labor of love, a prized early venture shared with his father in a touching enthusiasm of mutual excitement, undertaken together.

I had read that Carl Jung intended Böllingen to be archaic: there was no telephone, electricity, or running water, no master plan. It was a return to a simpler life where he surrounded himself with symbols of the past, as in the stone tablets he carved with the names of his antecedents and their family crest, another stone with an alchemical saying in Latin, and a third with a mandala of Jung's own design. And if the completed house resembled a fairy tale castle, this was more accidental than intentional. Franz discussed some of his thoughts about Böllingen when he was a willing teenager invited by his father to help with the early construction of the building project in 1923 and 1927, and later as a professional architect who prepared the plans and construction of the additions in

1931 and 1935, and again in 1955, helping to construct a second story to the 1927 tower.

His father's process of building at Bollingen lasted over a period of thirty-two years! It was difficult for Franz to describe this to me because of his own ideas of what a house might be, and he did so hesitantly, but also clearly wanting his part to be understood. The Bollingen Tower property, I realized, was multi-faceted. And I discovered it was a subtle, tender mixture of pride and nostalgia, perhaps, and also, for Franz, a set of professional contradictions and exasperations. That story evolved as the afternoon progressed. Before long, I was surprised when he threw up his hands at one point and called the Bollingen structure "the mole's heap."

He had matured, graduated from university, and entered into an architecture profession. There was a time, and Bollingen probably the place, that made him call the retreat the mole's heap, as if describing a set of contradictions for himself. I did not ask questions, but let things move as they would.

In a lighter vein, Franz told a story about this wondrous house wherein we sat and an incident when his younger sister Lil was celebrating her fifth birthday. The story has it that her father, the eminent Dr. Carl Jung, stopped on the way home from work and bought a birthday cake for her at a local bakery. Upon presenting the gift to his little girl, she opened the box, observed the glorious confection, and cried out, "Mother!! Franz's father brought me a CAKE!" Franz said, "We all had to explain to her that Franz's father was her father too!" He also told a story from a few years later. As a young man, at age seventeen or eighteen, he acquired a motorcycle. Franz managed to keep this a secret from his parents, knowing they would fear for his safety and most likely would not approve. Somehow, his favorite aunt, his mother's sister Margaret, agreed to let him store it at her place. He suddenly turned and spoke to me directly, "Don't you think it a bit strange that a young man should have and own a motorcycle without his parents knowing? But it was a very busy house!" he added. He also had a fine tweed suit, of which he was quite proud, and one day, alas, there was the inevitable accident, where both suit and motorcycle came to an unfortunate and irrevocable end. The young owner escaped and managed to survive the tragedy with only a skinned knee. The favorite aunt, sworn to secrecy, bandaged the knee. Some two or three months later, Mother Emma asked whatever happened to the nice tweed suit, and solemn son said something about having outgrown it and hadn't Mother noticed how tall he had become? And then he mentioned that he had given away the suit to some shorter fellow that really needed it, since it no longer was "suit-able!" Somehow, Mother accepted the tale. But then, it was a "very busy house!" as he again emphasized.

Franz then began the story of meeting Lilly, his true love, and later, his wife. As he matured into young manhood, it was customary for the neighborhood friends, with whom Franz had grown up, to have dance parties almost weekly at the homes of those who had houses and gardens large enough. They danced to the music of phonograph records and served sandwiches, sweets, fruits, and punch with a little wine. He said, "So to dance. Ah, yes. Having four sisters, it was important socially that I should dance. Besides, I really loved dancing!" Franz's sister Helene, or Lil, as he called her, had decided it was time for them to take their turn and prepare a party at Seestrasse #228 for local friends. Lil invited a friend from Baden, Lilly Merker, and suggested she spend the night with them in Küsnacht after the party. Another male friend, a cousin in the Merker clan, came along as a sort of Merker family representative for the outing and to watch out for young Lilly. The evening arrived and Franz was in the family kitchen, fixing punch and wearing a white linen jacket, when Lilly walked by and spotted him from the doorway. The story she later told Franz is that she thought, "What a nice handsome *kelner*"—or in English, waiter—"the Jungs have hired for the occasion!" At that time, Lil thought Franz was still courting his sweetheart of nearly five years, unaware the romance had ended. Before the party, she had asked Franz to dance with Lilly at least twice since Lilly knew no one there except her Merker cousin. Franz had agreed. Both Franz and Lilly were tall and made a splendid pair as both liked to dance and were very good at it. The Schottische and other favorite popular Swiss dances were irresistible to Franz. He simply had to dance—and with Lilly! In the morning, his sister Lil scolded him for leading this young woman guest astray by monopolizing her attention all evening, not realizing Franz was very interested in the tall, sweet, and shy young woman from Baden. Franz borrowed the family car and along with Lil and the Merker cousin, drove Lilly home to Baden. Lilly's mother was relieved to see them as she had been uneasy regarding the overnight arrangement. As Franz told this charming tale, he demonstrated some dance steps from an elegant waltz, which he hummed. I could almost hear phonograph music floating in the air as I pictured this tender scene from his youth. He does not dance now. When I asked him why, he said it made him tired, and he stopped abruptly. He said he had first taken dance lessons at the Hotel Sonne, at age twelve or thirteen. Later, he entered the gymnasium in Zurich and attended dancing classes there as well. Franz also talked of his earlier professional choices. He had made an effort to undertake medical studies, but after eighteen months, he felt the need to "separate myself further from my father." I sensed there must have been an experience in this story of crucial importance and decision-making, not without considerable tension and heartache. But

I did not question him further, and we did not discuss it. What seemed to make him comfortable was reminiscing.

Shortly after that time, he was called for a year of military service, which was required of all young men in Switzerland. Later, with relief and pleasure, he began his studies in Stuttgart at the University, preparing himself to become an architect. He added, quite calmly, "My Lilly . . . " and described the marriage as "Two trees growing separately, with common roots and branches inter-twining." Lilly began extensive studies in philosophy after their marriage. He recalled that she tried, once, to engage him in the Kant dialectic, but he was unable or unwilling to venture there.

He mentioned Lilly also did twenty years of Jungian analysis with Dr. Mary Louise Von Franz, who had said that this set them apart, somewhat, meaning there was a difference in the manner in which he and Lilly related. I added, "Which is not uncommon among marriages when one member undertakes analysis and the other does not." He added, "Her thirst for knowledge was boundless." While remembering this, he told another tale. He said there were food problems for Lilly as the boys grew up. Of their four sons, "The two oldest sons would eat no meat; the younger, no fish or chicken; and I eat nothing from the inside of an animal, like the liver or kidney." "Poor Lilly," he moaned. I assumed Lilly did all the cooking and sympathized, having managed a busy kitchen throughout my marriage, especially during the early years while raising children. "Later on," he continued, "the older boys liked rare steak, and the younger ones the steak black outside and inside!" He shrugged, slightly, as if demonstrating how frustrating it must have been for his wife. After reminiscing in this manner, he added, thoughtfully, "I always tried to offer Lilly as much freedom as was possible. As an architect, I knew there was always more than one solution to any problem, and I must be ready to think again. I think I was a good husband."

A noise came from downstairs, and his expression became troubled. "Lorenz is barely able to manage the stairs, he is so out of breath. Verena helped him pack yesterday." I understood he was speaking of his visiting son who was severely ill. I saw the anxiety in his face. But we did not speak further on this. Franz was quiet for a few moments, immersed in his anxiety about his son, but not willing, or able, to speak of it further. Soon he continued with his train of thoughts about earlier family stories. Then came a big story as it related to him. "One evening, before my father died, he called me to his bedside and told me to go to the cellar and bring up a bottle of good wine. He wanted to tell me something. So of course I did and we enjoyed the wine. After a few minutes, Father said, 'Wait until I die. I want to tell you, then, after I am gone, something wonderful will happen to you.' Of course I begged him to tell me, and he would not. 'Just wait,' he said and added, 'something you can't even imagine.' I decided this was his way of helping me get through the hard times ahead. From a young age, I had learned how to handle the family sail boat. I always sailed Dad up to Böllingen in our boat. Ours had to be small in order to go under the Rapperswill Bridge between the Küsnacht house and my father's Böllingen retreat. In the late 1930s, I learned about bigger and better sailboats, but had forgotten about them because sailing, for me then, was about taking Dad up to Böllingen.

"After the boys came along, I sailed with the two older ones, and we had a fine time. I taught both of them how to handle the boat. But Lilly didn't like being left behind with the younger boys while I and the two older ones went off sailing. Sometime after my father died, I told Lilly the boat was getting old, and I should replace it, and she said, 'Franz, why don't you get a real sail boat?' I was stunned. Then I said, very slowly, 'What's that you say, Wife?' She replied that I no longer needed to worry about getting under the Rapperswill Bridge, and we could have a great boat, and all six of us could sleep on it, and I could teach all the boys how to handle a real boat. It was a huge idea. It had never occurred to me that I could do such a thing. So after many unsuccessful starts and stops, I, myself, finally designed the boat we wanted—a yawl, two masts, that could sleep eight! We named her the Andromeda and launched her in Amsterdam in 1964. We learned to sail the great Mediterranean together." He shook his head, seemingly lost in this incredible memory. "We enjoyed her for ten years," he concluded, softly. I nodded, quietly, unwilling to interrupt this fine memory. There was a long pause as he remembered those joyous days for himself. Then he said, "That turned out to be the thing my father meant when he told me that something wonderful would happen after he died."

After this story, we both grew quiet. I finally noticed it was nearly eight o'clock and prepared to leave. We walked down the silent stairs to the front door. He stopped, turned, and looked straight at me. "My father, my mother, and my wife lived and died in this house," he said, quietly. He spoke with a stark, yet tender sadness. I gathered it in me, as best I could, and nodded. "Yes," I said. Then, much to my astonishment, Franz invited me to visit Böllingen the following Monday, along with his lady friend, Els Glasser. Stunned, I hesitated, staring at him. I could hardly believe his words. Finally, I said, "Franz, I would love this. Thank you." He nodded and opened the door for me. As I walked through the dark under the street lamps, I relived the moods of the evening, a huge jumble of delight, conjecture, memory, sympathy, sadness, followed by astonishment at what I had heard, seen, and shared, and surges of excitement mixed with joy and confusion, at once all combined to become a moment-in-time, unlike any other. The evening had been like a huge jolt into some other world. A stillness settled over me. Even now, as I rekindle this memory, I can close my eyes and recall that fine moment of complete and total surprise. I walked a long time. Finally, the church tower began to strike. I could hardly believe it was eight o'clock. And amid all these sensations, I felt deeply pleased, and very alive in the simple truth and honesty of this encounter. I found a quiet restaurant and scribbled notes.

CHAPTER FOUR

BÖLLINGEN TOWER,
JANUARY 30, 1989

❋

WE DROVE TO BÖLLINGEN ACCOMPANIED BY FRANZ'S LADY FRIEND, Els Glasser, who was to become a warm and delightful friend. During the drive, Franz spoke at length of various styles of Swiss architecture, how chalets were first built and how good barns were constructed vertically so they would settle on the land properly and accommodate the storage of winter food. He also explained the original purpose of half-timber construction. All of this was done with a flow of narrative on his part as he pointed out buildings along the way to illustrate one or another of his explanations. Carl Jung's famous Böllingen retreat, which is only a short distance from the town of Böllingen itself, sits back from the road, but is not hard to identify because of the three towers visible from nearby. We parked and walked to the front entrance through the damp and overcast winter morning.

It was very quiet. Franz, carrying a huge ring of keys, strode ahead of Els and me. He had explained that every shutter was closed and locked for the winter from the inside, and he wanted us to see the views from each window as we went from room to room. He told us his plan was to progress through the sections of the buildings in the order they were constructed, beginning with 1923. Franz was then age fourteen and had been an eager helper. Inside the first and earliest building, I stood in a kitchen, suddenly remembering a tale from Carl Jung's own fanciful description in *Memories, Dreams, Reflections* of the "lares and penates" as sleeping ghosts of the kitchen tools that must be respectfully attended to when cooking because of the long time they had been left silent and unused. I saw a small solid table and noticed the African-style circular stairway of the tower, of which I had also read. There was a sturdy rope, probably suspended from an overhead beam in the tower that, as Franz explained, gave stability to the climber since the stair space was too narrow for a railing. Franz grasped the rope and started up the narrow stairs, using the rope for balance with a sense of familiarity. From the second floor he dropped the rope and called down for me to follow suit and take hold of it to stabilize my climb upward. I still remember the feel of the hefty rope in my hands as he encouraged me from the top of the stairs. After I stood firmly on the second floor, he dropped the rope for Els. Upstairs, the first room, Franz said, was for storage. He led the way into a second room where I quickly met the yellow, brownish orange, and white tones of the famous Philemon image, painted by Carl Jung, on the inside wall's wooden surface. I recalled Dr. Jung had named Philemon his guide, a man from New Testament biblical texts beloved by the apostles Paul and Timothy. The figure of Philemon appeared to Jung in a dream in 1913. I recognized the painting because copies of this image appear in several books about Carl Jung. But seeing Jung's original painting in this very intimate, almost primal setting spoke to me of his serious and private thinking, and perhaps recording dreams, sometime, years and years ago. Franz unlocked the attractive Swiss shutters of this room, and I took in the misty view. For a moment, it seemed as though I was alone inside a medieval castle, peering far off into the mist, as if waiting to see a horse-bound rider come galloping toward us. When I turned back to the room, I noticed the uneven feel of the floor and a small table with one chair. We passed into a second upstairs room that Franz named "the children's room." I wondered if Franz had slept there on occasion as a child or as a young helper as the building progressed. Franz invited me to check the view from this second window in the tower, and after I did so, and admired the still misty view, I turned back to the larger room and took a step or two. Franz and Els had moved ahead and started down the curving staircase.

As I turned toward the stairs, I was met with a great surprise. I was faced by an enormous, stunning, blue-and-white star. It was painted on an inside corner wall, close to the stairway. I stood stricken, almost dumbfounded, by the star's majesty and incredible power. I had neither read nor heard of this wall painting! Franz later said he thought it had never been photographed as the light is poor, and the distance from wall to camera would not be enough to get a good picture and do it justice. This was the only moment when I was completely alone during this trip to Bollingen, and it was also the moment in which I felt closest to the singular spirit of Carl Jung. Such glory in such a small and private corner. I remained there for a time, imagined Carl Jung standing just there, painting an image of such incredible symmetry and mystery in this silent, narrow space and thought of how he must have needed, for himself, to paint this glorious star on this particular wall. It seemed to me an act of highly personal spiritual intensity. Even now, I think of it as my own special surprise, maybe a symbol for me of the hidden power of Bollingen. I have never forgotten it. A truly wondrous star, so close. In succeeding years, when I'd again hear Carl Jung's response to the question of whether he believed in God—"I don't need to believe; I know"—I think of this star. I had wondered if it was called "Aimalee's Star" because I found these words along the margin of my original notes where I'd scribbled them. But I wasn't sure of the spelling, nor who the name referenced—perhaps Jung's mother, Emilie Jung, who died in 1921. But for me, the painting remains the "Böllingen Star." Maybe someday I will know! In the meantime, I will simply recall it with awe and a certain feeling of powerful mystique. It spoke to me of the early days before the rest of the retreat was built, when Jung went there alone. I believe *Septem Sermones Ad Mortuous* was written there, early in his writing years. But of that I am not entirely certain. Such glory in such a small space; yet still, entirely personal.

After a long moment and almost in a sort of trance, I followed Franz and Els down the stairs. I remember I moved very slowly, carefully, back down, down, down the narrow stairs, grasping the rope, wanting to retain the image of the star for as long as I could, to gather my thoughts, and maintain my perilous balance in the descent. Franz and Els were waiting quietly for me. Franz then pointed out and described his father's use of the stone carving tools hanging on the inside wall by the doorway, with which he chiseled the wonderful lines, phrases, dates, and family names, one by one, on the stone surfaces and corners of the outside courtyard wall. He went on to explain the different kinds of chisels and mallets used for stone cutting. Smiling gently at the memory, he said he had often carried and held these tools for his father when, over the years, Dr. Jung chiseled names and dates on the stone's surfaces. Sensing my ignorance and holding a rather small wooden mallet in his hand, Franz demonstrated that when chiseling on some kinds of stone, this particular kind of supple, wooden mallet is best. He said caution is necessary when working on softer stones to avoid unwanted chipping, which is why they used the lighter wooden mallet.

His patient explanation of tools seemed at the time a strange combination with touring the towers, but I have never forgotten it, and realize now that it does serve as a metaphor for the management of delicate memories for this book, a seeming insurmountable task with all these papers and letters and notes strewn around. It follows to think of all my notes as being stones that require careful sorting and study, the work refusing to be rushed. The "wooden mallet" part of this project is the computer itself, upon which arthritic fingers move slowly, slowly along . . . tap, tap . . . gently, one by one . . . on my own slim resources to accomplish this task. And so, I work in my old age to bring to life the story of Franz and the others at Böllingen.

Franz bounded up and down the stairs, opening shutters, letting the light flow inside. He explained this addition that solved that problem, this staircase, that special view of the lake, this intention, that outcome . . . all with such recall and seeming pleasure that I began to sense what actual real delight and challenge he had experienced here.

Now he stepped from the doorway that opened to the courtyard and paused to say that at one time, this doorway opened to a view of the lake, and people liked to draw a chair out on a fine day to enjoy the sunshine on the water. He led Els and me through a doorway into the second tower and another staircase. Franz again bounded up these stairs and into a large library, crossed the room to unlock shutters and reveal a view of the still misty lake. Light flowed inside. He indicated we seat ourselves in comfortable chairs, mine with a view of the lake. This second section, Franz told us, was begun when he was finishing up his credentials as an architect. He pointed out an oriental screen piece above the stairway, the library shelves, and guest rooms. This section was harmony and balance, and was a gracious addition. The third tower, which Franz designed, was completed in the late 1950s just three or four years before his father's death.

He showed us the connector he had designed for the third tower, the tower that his father asked him to design after he was an established architect. He explained the various problems and challenges he had experienced . . . this intention, that outcome . . . all with such meticulous detail that I could sense what actual delight and challenge he had experienced here. We paused in the doorway as he explained how this third addition solved the problem of needing extra rooms for visitors, speakers, and family meetings. His voice reflected a genuine joy and pride in working with his father. It began to reveal to me how in this attainment, this sharing a building process over the years, Franz and his father were bound together as much, perhaps more than at any other time during Jung's later life. We did not visit the meditation room that remains closed to all visitors as Franz explained. I passed the closed door, feeling a respectful sense of Jung's need for privacy and for the vast distances of the human spirit he must have traveled behind those doors.

The third tower is the one that gives the house its splendid symmetry as seen from the lake because this upper story rises above the other two towers and balances the aesthetic composition of the whole. Franz did not point this out to me; I only realized it as I studied a photograph of the house that Els Glasser later shared with me.

The photograph was taken from the water's edge with a view of the entire structure and helped me understand the unifying symmetry of the tower as it rises above the other two towers and balances the aesthetic image of the entire composition. I remembered Carl Jung writing how, to still his grief over Emma's death, he began to build. "I suddenly realized that the small central section which crouched so low, so hidden, was myself! I could no longer hide myself behind the "maternal" and the "spiritual towers." The result of his understanding was a tall, striking, half-timbered upper story that dominated the two towers and successfully completed the composition. Jung was quick to admit that he was not immediately aware of this symbolism. "During the building work, of course, I never considered these matters. I built the house in sections, always following the concrete needs of the moment. It might also be said that I built it in a kind of dream."

I still recall some of the particular wall hangings of fabric and canvas within the towers and remember seeing a strange Eastern-style picture of a human form lying on a floor, wrapped in shroud linens, while rows of attendants appear to be in prayer or meditation, all dressed in similar white garments and placed in symmetrical precision on either side of the body, all kneeling in exactly the same position. This seemed to me to be a respectful ceremonial practice for a distinguished person or family member, reminiscent of a foreign tradition. For some reason, this image is very clear in my mind, although there were many pictures and wall hangings, including a picture of Erasmus somewhere. I also recall a mounted metal fish with a ruby red stone for an eye! That red eye has remained with me over the years. Franz pointed these out as we were sitting in the comfortable library chairs, also pointing out various details, including the second staircase problem skillfully solved, all with such meticulous recall and obvious pleasure that I could actually sense what proprietary delight and challenge he had experienced here over the years, as well as the many frustrations with his father's instructions and small changes along the way. He shared all this with an unmistakable level of genuine and personal pride. He also explained how the great green tile stove, there in the library, must be heated slowly for a couple of days, with very small fires if it has been sitting cold for a long time, and how difficult it was to bring the stove up in pieces and assemble it in the room. It was, of course, cold in this January weather, but we were not terribly uncomfortable.

The rooms directly above the library were built in 1955, and he took pleasure in telling me the stories of the rooms' designs, the problems inherent in constructing this and that part. He said this library was the space he liked best, next to the round tower that he built with his father when he was fifteen years old. He said, "You see each stone and think, yes, I put this one here." He also spoke of the current uses for this library chamber, including private meetings for family members and for the occasional guest speakers and visitors. Later, I also remembered the shutters and their usefulness in deferring the cold weather, and the fine view of the misty lake.

We went down the stairs again and out into the courtyard to visit the stone carvings: the famous Bollingen stone, the alchemical pictures, the tribute to Emma, and the list of family members and ancestors. It was at this juncture that I was able to grasp something of the physical strength and stamina of Carl Jung, the man, as I moved from stone to inscribed stone, each one so artistically and carefully wrought, seeing the carefully chiseled names of generations of the Jung family forever inscribed. The muscles of my back and arms began to ache and twitch as I realized what must have been required in order to present so permanent a set of messages to his descendants, both familial and spiritual. Later, I wrote in my journal, "If ever any woman had a personal concretized animus experience or incredible constellation, I have had one!"

•

Now, as I write some thirty years later, I wonder if the names and dates of new family members have been added or if the chiseled and hammered rolls have been kept as Dr. Jung left them. Franz shared the stories of the building with me through the history of the creation of the entirety—this stone, that carving, this staircase, that painting, giving me his strange mixture of pride, mystery, and aesthetic criticism like a great good giant guide, sensate and sensible. He bounded up and down the stairs, letting light inside with a sort of proprietary pleasure. He moved with great strides of confidence, even identifying the years and his own ages during which each addition and change was made. As I recall this, I compare the energy of this experience to my own childhood images of the biblical story of Adam giving names to everything in his Garden of Eden.

•

Els brought me the visitor's book to sign, which I did, with some trepidation at first and then with a sense of simple gratitude at being invited to this unexpected adventure. I experienced both father and son in new ways as a result of this extraordinary and unexpected visit to Carl Jung's Böllingen retreat. Jung's desire for a place where he could be alone to work implied his family household of six children must have, understandably, left little space for privacy. As I looked over the dates of the children's births, it seemed that for the first ten or twelve years of Carl Jung's marriage, his wife, Emma, was probably either pregnant or nursing little ones, all of which implies a busy atmosphere at the least and a singular need by a scholarly man for solitude. Another fact I learned was that Carl Jung purchased the property that became the Böllingen retreat land, some thirty miles from his home in Küsnacht, just two months after his mother's death. The town of Böllingen was the land area in which his mother had grown up. These additional biographical pieces have helped ground me in my sense that Carl Jung's concept of God began in his experiences with his mother, and he produced that private and glorious star mandala as a tribute to her.

I found this note in an early notebook from years ago: "I must find out more about Aimalee's Star." As discussed above, that mystery unraveled over the years as I read further into the many books about Carl Jung's work and life. It took me a long time to figure out that Aimalie must have been Carl Jung's mother, Emilie. Another piece of information written by biographers gave me her background, coming from a household where generations had been involved in spiritual thinking, both as clergy and laypeople, possessing various belief factors.

•

We walked through the quiet winter woods, smelling of hoar frost and sweet, damp leaves, to the edge of the lake where tall grass grew and whispered in the wind. A small sailboat was moored silently, close to the reeds but still in the water. This image, too, remains with me after all these years; how quietly the little boat sat there, its bare mast like a sort of sentinel through the winter, alone in the quiet memory of this place. It reminded me of the stories of Franz sailing his father up to Bollingen, years and years ago.

I picked up a little white stone from the lakeside and asked Franz if I might keep it. He nodded and smiled. To shut the gate was a long and lasting moment. The tears come now as I write this story. My heart was then, and is now, this moment, like a great sponge.

Through the natural grace of Franz's guidance, I was given the opportunity to see the Bollingen towers through his eyes and his particular appraisal. Also, I was singularly blessed with the gentle help of Els Glasser, without whom I am sure this would not have happened. But what remained for me, even after so many years, was that Franz definitely, unmistakably, went to great lengths to ensure that I actually saw this place under his direction. Somehow, from the beginning, he had trusted me to do a thorough job telling his story. The story continues, under its own power.

CHAPTER FIVE

ALONG THE WAY

✳

MUCH TO MY SURPRISE, FRANZ HAD TWO MORE STOPS PLANNED FOR the afternoon. The first was a superb specimen of early Swiss half-timber architecture near Hombrechticon—the Elighaus. Franz parked near the massive building and explained it was built in the year 1625 and was still in use as a dwelling. It was, indeed, a monumental and worthy example, and quite alien to the manner of half-timber design I was familiar with in a style known as Tudor in neatly kept neighborhoods in Kansas City.

The second stop was another surprise. Franz had carefully planned to visit a gracious, contemporary home of his design built in 1984 for his son Peter, his wife Olga, and their children. Franz wanted me to see this rich, contrasting side of his work, uniquely and entirely different from the Böllingen experience. It was stunning, indeed, representing some forty years between the Böllingen structures and this contemporary architectural achievement. The house sits like a fine ship on a hillside near a lake, in harmony with the land. While taking in this delightful spectacle, Peter's wife, Olga, walked out, greeted us cordially, and invited us in for coffee and croissants. It was clear our visit was no surprise to her, only to me. Olga was a refined and cordial hostess. She spoke of their daughter, attending school at Vanderbilt in Nashville, Tennessee, and of other family members. Whenever she lapsed into her comfortable and elegantly spoken German, I could sense Franz and Els stiffen a little, and gently steer her back into the courtesy of speaking English for my sake. I thanked her, apologetically, aware of my limited vocabulary. We soon became comfortable, often combining both languages when making a point or exclamation for each other. She invited us to tour more of the fine large rooms, the gracious French doors in the living room overlooking the landscape, a generous library, a handsome paneled dining room with a gracious design of fruit and flowers carved and polished in the paneling over the sideboard. I caught a glimpse of an adjoining greenhouse where lush pots of camellias bloomed and admired once again how beautifully the house lay on the land. Not far from the house, there was an extraordinary outdoor feature of water and rock formation and the home of Peter's favorite pets—a family of land tortoises. Franz pointed out the four chimneys, and Els added that each bedroom had its own bath. Franz's careful work reflected his energy, present in both places, in very different and unique ways. I could not make the transition from Böllingen's towers to Peter's house without noting the inherent contrasts, which I am sure Franz intended. Later, I recalled it had to do with an almost infinite attention to detail and a sort of harmony within itself, considering the contrasts of time and circumstance each represented. I hoped the notes I made and the visual images and feelings I carried with me would help me record and do justice to what had unfolded, almost as if he were saying, "Böllingen and this home are still not all there is to me!"

As we prepared to leave, I thanked Olga for her hospitable welcome and bade her to call me the next time she would be in the United States to visit her daughter at Vanderbilt. On the return trip to Küsnacht, Franz missed the intended turn as he was responding to my rapid-fire questions about his work. Finally, I realized I needed to cease jabbering so he could find our way home. It seemed all three of us were excited by the day's adventures. When we reached Küsnacht, I invited them to dine with me in a restaurant of their choice in reciprocation for the day's pleasures. They resorted to rapid-fire German and came to a consensus: rather than an elegant dinner out, would I agree to dinner Wednesday evening, chez Frau Glasser. We could then talk comfortably in private of American architecture in the Midwest. At his suggestion, I recalled two books containing photos of Frank Lloyd Wright's Kansas City homes and buildings that I had purchased and brought with me to Küsnacht for Franz. Even at that quick moment, I knew Frank Lloyd Wright's Community Christian Church, on the Plaza in Kansas City, would be pleasant to discuss. All this flowed quickly through my mind.

•

The following Wednesday, at the home of Els Glasser, we three were at our most relaxed, comfortable selves, people of the world enjoying our mutual interests, good conversation, fine food, and the pleasure of each other's company and companionship. I had also brought a copy of my paper on Emma's letters to Freud, which pleased him.

Franz told us a charming story involving his older sister Gret that occurred when he was nineteen and Gret was twenty. On Carnival Night, they dressed up and attended, in complete masked disguise, a party for the psychological society and assorted guests. After many teasings from guests regarding the obviously young guests, they were finally recognized by their parents who kept the others ignorant about their identity. Carl suggested Franz sort of sidle up to tease Herman Hesse, a friend of the society, and pointed him out as a famous author. Carl whispered the first name of a certain woman he knew about and mentioned that Franz might go up to Hesse and whisper her name with a sort of question implied. When Franz did so, poor Herr Hess was brought to complete confusion and consternation since his interest in this woman was highly confidential. Herr Hesse coughed, sputtered, and spilled his drink while the young masked guest moved away. It took quite a few minutes for Herr Hesse to recover, while onlookers wondered what on earth had happened. Carl apparently enjoyed the joke, and the young masked guests moved along to others, until, following Father's orders, they left in short order.

Franz had prefaced this story, saying he and Gret liked to enjoy pranks from time to time on parents and friends.

Franz followed this with another story, this about his sister Agathe meeting an American at a dinner party. The man said, "You may call me Bill," to which she replied most formally, "And you may call me Grandmother." This amused Franz enormously. The story illustrated how extroverted most Americans seem to the Swiss, particularly with the social use of first names with new friends or just people they know minimally.

Another story followed. Franz and Lilly often visited the Mueller Castle near Garmisch, an interesting gathering place for stimulating conversation. Guests at the various private dinner parties were not allowed to disclose their occupations, titles, or proper names, and were seated at mealtimes by their host and hostess to enjoy conversations with other unknown guests. This wonderful and interesting custom did not survive World War II. These visits were in the early years of their marriage. Franz completed his studies in 1937 and married Lilly in November of that year, so these visits coincided with those early years. I also learned that night that Carl Jung's *The Red Book* was kept in a vault of "some other place of safety," as Franz described it.

Els paid me a direct compliment, saying she thought I had "a warm heart." I was embarrassed, surprised, somewhat flustered, but thanked her, and replied, "In America we have the phrase: it takes one to know one." So there we were, three warm hearts in the midst of creatively sharing the ideas and images that enrich our lives in vastly different parts of the world. After a pleasant meal, we sat in Els's comfortable living room. She asked if I knew what it was that pleased them about me, a question I had been semi-consciously carrying. This was an unexpected surprise. I had wondered and would have liked to know, but would certainly never have asked. She said the thing they most liked about me and felt comforted by was the "clarity of my speech." Franz smiled and added, "Yes, that is what it is. So many Americans are difficult to understand and have such different dialects." Franz added something about me being like his mother, and Els nodded with a slight sound of agreement. I had not associated these facts. It is true that I felt comfortable when talking to German-speaking people. And then I realized that this ability and interest of mine had begun long before Franz Jung entered my life.

•

I heard the kind comments of Franz and Els, embarrassed somewhat, but I accepted them as graciously as I could. Much later that evening, and several times since, I have reflected on this very issue. When I have had to face the task of returning to the writing of this tale and completing it, I have thought it would be natural for people who may be reading this to wonder how it was that Franz Jung and Els Glasser decided they liked me, felt safe talking to me and sharing their story, and going to considerable effort to arrange that I might actually see a portion of Franz's work. At some point, readers might wonder, as I wondered, why me? Why, indeed? I began, while writing this, to try to bring together some of the experiences of my own life that readers might need to know so as to understand the answer to the question. When I arranged a visit to the Seestrasse home of Carl Jung, I had no idea there was a serious book in my mind. As I recall the evening in Els's living room, I had not realized what, indeed, kept this story evolving. But there was one simple comment she made and dropped suddenly. Els said Franz had mentioned that when he is with me and we are talking, there is something that reminds him, in my manner of speaking, of his own mother, Emma; there is a distinctly feminine quality to my voice that pleases him. I recall quickly brushing aside her comment because it somewhat embarrassed me.

There were reasons why I reminded Franz of his mother that occurred to me from time to time, some of which had to do with my feeling of closeness with my own children. The idea, for me at first, seemed outrageous because my feelings about Frau Jung were rather like a distant respect. I knew she had been a very busy mother. As had I. I knew from other texts that she was highly thought of by the Jungian community. At one time during my correspondence with Franz, I mentioned that my Jungian study group was working on the letters Emma wrote to Sigmund Freud. I believe there were five. Franz replied he had not heard about these letters and asked if I would send copies of them to him, so I did, making copies from my husband's collection of the Freud / Jung letters and sending them off.

Another part had to do with my familiarity with German-speaking people as a result of a writing assignment I carried out when I was eighteen years old and living with my father and mother in Stuttgart shortly after World War II, in 1946–47. Actually, it started even earlier, when I was fifteen years old, writing a weekly unfinished story for children that was published in a newspaper in Flint, Michigan. I am certain this seems a strange thing, but to me it seemed perfectly natural. My mother's brother, Uncle Pete, was a writer and editor of *The Flint Journal*. It was a fine paper and carried a weekly page devoted to children, "The Wide Awake Club." The object was to introduce and encourage schoolchildren in the skills of reading, writing, and drawing cartoons and pictures. This paper had a wide readership, and Uncle Pete and Mom decided I could write a weekly unfinished story; I would think up a situation or a tangle of some sort, show it to Mom and make changes if she suggested them, and then mail my unfinished story to *The Flint Journal* in care of a lady named Mary Rowen, whom I never met. The paper published a story every Saturday, and schoolchildren would write and send in a solution to the story. Mary Rowen would choose two "good endings" from those sent in and publish them above the next unfinished story the following week, along with the names of the contestants. It was the goal of the newspaper to encourage youngsters to write and draw pictures, and it was very popular with good local participation. I was also given a little salary; I think it was $3.50 per story, so every month I got a check for about $15.00, which was a handsome amount at the time. I spent most of it on patterns and material for making clothes for myself once I learned to manage a sewing machine. My girlfriend and I would ride our bikes to Plainfield on Friday afternoons and pick out the patterns and cloth for whatever we decided to make, and we would pin and cut and stitch away the evening and the next day finish our outfits and attend the "Swing Lobby" at the YMCA! We were living near an Army base in New Jersey.

Dad was sent to Germany and we followed, sailing on a huge troop ship before transferring onto a train for Stuttgart where Dad was stationed. As sad as I was to leave my high school friends, the trip on the boat to Europe was, indeed, delightful. We had a room with double-decker beds. Quite by accident, I met the sergeant who was in charge of the music recordings on the ship. His name was Cass Lackey. He asked me if there were songs I would like to hear. I told him a few titles. After that, he invited me to join him in choosing the recordings the troops would hear. He even let me introduce them. I remember playing "Paper Doll" by Frank Sinatra. So then, whenever I was walking on the deck, the soldiers would yell, "Hey, girl, how about more Frank Sinatra?"—or other artists.

Evenings, we met in a mess hall for bingo. Once I won a box of cigars, which I gave away one by one. The soldiers would call to me, "Hey, Mary Dian, how about a cigar?" I had a good time, and it helped me recover from having to leave my school before graduation.

Once in Germany, Uncle Pete and Mom put their heads together again and decided I would write a column from Germany for "The Wide Awake Club," only this would be in letter form for a teenage audience. I would interview German teenagers, or sometimes older people. The pen name I chose for myself was Jud, the name of one of my cousins, and I mailed a "Dear Jud" letter every Wednesday from Germany. The mail took about two weeks to get across the ocean at that time.

I remember many interesting conversations with young Germans, when we could find an interpreter (usually a teacher) or an adult German who worked around the Army base and knew some English. This explains, then, that talking to German-speaking people, listening to their stories, and writing about them was a normal part of my life. This may help readers understand more of the "why" of my encounter with Franz, which lasted for several years, ending at the time of Franz's death in January of 1963.

•

When one becomes as old as I am now, it is customary to try and figure out some of the different paths working within one's life. But as I recall that evening in Küsnacht, in Els's living room, I now understand I had not grasped what, indeed, kept this story evolving. Somehow, circumstances completely out of my reasoning on the "why" of things joined me, if only briefly, to the story of Franz Jung's family. As I was a younger adult, it was clear they were generously sharing their story with me and going to considerable effort to see that I actually saw a portion of Franz's work. But ideas about "why," I find, shed very little light on the enormous "WHY" of things. Now, as a practicing psychotherapist, a former teacher, a school administrator, a public television executive, and a mother of adults with families of their own, I am apt to try to steer away, at least at first, from the "why" of things, and settle on the "what now."

Adding what few facts about my life fit into this tale, I shall continue as best I can, starting with "clarity of my speech." I owe that to years of violin tuning and playing enough music to learn how to listen seriously. Also, as I've written before, I lived for a time in Stuttgart, Germany, and wrote stories about German people. I recall having my seventeenth birthday in the Graf Zeppelin Hotel. As for speech-giving, being President of many groups over the years and being extroverted enough to enjoy public speaking fills in that "why."

Why, then, did Franz Jung decide to share some of the deeply personal feelings and events of his life with me? I have thought about this carefully as the pieces came together for this manuscript. But that evening, in Els's comfortable living room, Franz and Els kindly tried to explain something of this to me. My later reckoning went something like this: First, they understood my speaking voice; second, they trusted me with their story. The first part about my voice is fairly easy to understand given the details of my own story. It is true I learned to listen carefully and produce, on paper, what I learned. These are skills that I sort of picked up along the pike. I also picked up speaking, listening, and writing skills alongside various members of my family, mostly my mother and Uncle Pete, both accomplished writers and journalists. Since Dad was an Army officer, we moved around often. We lived in Detroit and later in New Jersey. And then in Stuttgart, Germany, a few months after the end of World War II. Uncle Pete and Mother kept me writing all that time.

Being understood is connected deeply to accurate hearing, and listening and responding. Has that been different for me than for others? How did I learn listening? Ah! I learned it from Mr. Keppley, my violin teacher, who built a quarter-sized fiddle for me when I was only five years old and gave me violin lessons in the sitting room behind his shop until I was ten years old. Early on, I had to learn how to tune that sensitive little violin instrument accurately to a very subtle intonation of what I later learned was called a "four forty A"—the tuning used by orchestras. Mr. Keppley would touch the "A" key on the piano in the lesson room, and I would tune my fiddle's "A" string with the peg, as Mr. Keppley showed me. Next I would tune the "E," then "D" and "G," and I was set to play, as they say, "in tune." Then I would touch the "A" key on our piano at home, and I could tune my violin by myself. Soon I could hear "A" in my head, just thinking about it, without the piano. I can still sing, by ear, a relatively accurate "A" tone, almost a "440A," like the first violinist gives at the beginning of a symphony concert, and all the other instruments then tune to it accordingly. I learned later that most string players can do this tuning by ear.

All else about Mr. Keppley that I remember is he had a little daughter, smaller than I was, but still close to my own age, about five years old. She would come into the practice room behind the store when I had my violin lesson if Mr. Keppley invited her. She would play whatever music I was playing. If we played well, we were each rewarded with a round piece of peppermint wrapped in paper, and we would clap for each other and celebrate! We learned how to mimic each other and copy what the other played.

Thanks to Mr. Keppley, peppermint, and his little daughter, my skill is not exactly what they call "perfect pitch" these days, but rather "relative pitch." This is why I hear the intonations of another's speaking voice and automatically, almost unconsciously, pitch my speaking pace and voice in a manner such that the other will hear, feel comfortable, and understand me. It is not so different a skill than tuning an instrument. Listening to one's self surely must have something to do with being understood and speaking clearly. From that acquired skill must have come the growth of a just-so story about listening and being listened to. So I have some sense of that part. I have called this my "trained ear," and it has served me well. The tuning of my ear has been a part of me, without ever knowing that not everyone can do this. And it might have something to do with speaking before audiences. It seems to me that even in casual conversation, to hear the intonations of another's voice and automatically calibrate and pitch and pace one's own voice does not seem so different from tuning an instrument.

Speaking to people is connected to hearing them when they talk, and making oneself understood by people who are much more comfortable using their own language, if indeed there are different languages being used, is almost as much about one's tone, intonation of feeling, and voice texture as it is about language differences—or so it seems to me. It is a matter of reading and hearing and reacting to words, feelings, and sounds. So I still hear fairly well, with some fairly specialized acuity and my tuning ear. Ergo, the knowing if I am being understood was pretty well refined before I even knew it. The tuning of my ear and watching the faces of those around me were parts of my skill set, if you will, and has been a part of me, without ever knowing that not everybody could do this. For me, it was just normal, like learning to tie one's shoes. It is important to add that I decided to major in music when I returned home from Germany and was ready for college. My mom and Uncle Pete thought they had groomed me for journalism, and they had. But what I didn't like about journalism was the constant push to write for deadlines and was haunted by Wednesday or Monday deadlines all my life it seemed! Maybe I just started too young to accept that part of the journalism world. But meeting and talking to strangers, and listening to their stories, and writing about them was always a big part of my life. I learned to train my ear and listen carefully, tried to understand and be understood as the young Germans struggled with their English, and I fumbled and stumbled with German. I developed a sense of story and a feeling of sensitivity to people who had lived through a terrible war. This is the best I can do, on the "why me" issue.

I realize now that I developed, in Stuttgart, what I call my "crack ear." When I talk to anyone who has a speech pattern or dialect different from mine, no matter what it is, I habitually lapse into a sort of reciprocal pattern, like an echo, of what the other person's ear wants, or feels comfortable answering. This, as mentioned, is a semi-conscious and almost instantaneous reflex piece of my own personhood, and I do not recall ever having been trained in this respect. During my many exchanges in Germany, I seemed to have been able to reply quickly, even to strangers, in their own rhythm of intonation, timing, and feeling, but not necessarily accurately in their own language. Actually, I never thought about this. It does occur to me that both Franz and I might be classified as extroverted among those readers who are cognizant of Jung's famed typologies, which might describe yet another piece of the "why" question that may arise. The extroverted piece might be described as a certain intuitive grasp of how one is being received and reciprocated in normal conversation. In Jungian parlance, it represents a combination of intuition and conversing with others. It seems to have been an intuitive response of mine for as long as I can remember and now, these many years later, mostly unconscious. Extroversion is described as: "A mode of psychological orientation where the movement of energy is toward the outer world." The rest of my life has been about music, marriage, home, raising a family, graduate schools, getting degrees, teaching, studying Jung, learning to listen and talk to all kinds of people as a practicing psychotherapist, and still writing!!!

We had to leave Germany after about six months because my Dad became very ill and needed to have treatment back in the States. We had planned to be in Germany for at least a year, so this was a big disappointment for me because, again, I didn't get to graduate with my class in Heidelberg. My class members, on the other hand, had their picture on the cover of *Life* magazine, wearing their Lederhosen.

•

I've tried to understand as best I could something of "why" the Franz work has developed and endured over these years. I am simply using my own ingrown sense of story and will try to see it to some sort of completion while the clock keeps on ticking. I am also cognizant, truthfully, that it became important to Franz that I recognize his work in as many manifestations as possible. Later still, I understood there had been a part of thinking and relaxing that seemed to have flourished best when he was with Els. I just happened to enter his life at a time when she deeply appreciated his story and his talents, and she was encouraging him to allow this to be identified and included in the family history.

As I gathered these fragments that night with Franz and Els, I understood Els really wanted me to record and write what was in his world. I gradually learned, later on, that she gave him the necessary ego strength to allow this to become a serious part of the record. A trio formed that day and remained intact for a substantial period of time, in fact, up until the time of Els's death. All of these things contributed both to my being easily understood by them and my omnipresent interest in story whenever it came my way. In truth, this remains, a journalism of sort.

Dear Frau Glasser,   *February 11, 1989*

What a delightful evening I enjoyed at your lovely home. It was extraordinarily kind of you to invite me to share a meal with you and your friend Franz Jung. I was immediately struck, upon meeting you, with your gentle spirit of quiet strength, and I am happy for you and Franz at the warmth and companionship that you bring to each other.

Also, I must thank you for helping me visit Böllingen. Your presence added much to that experience for me and brought a comforting touch of great feminine sweetness to that overpoweringly masculine world.

I send, along with my deep gratitude to you, another warm wish for an excellent birthday celebration next week.

Also, I shall send you some Kansas City Bar'B'Que sauce as promised!

Cordially, Mary Dian Molton

After I returned home from my trip to Switzerland and my visit with Franz and Els, I began to pick up little stories from the vast literature that had developed regarding Carl Jung's life, specifically illustrating something of the importance to him of having a son. These would have pleased Franz, had he read them, in the same manner that my first contact with him by letter pleased him. However, these sources are scarce. I am including a few recorded receptions of the news of Franz's birth in the early part of the twentieth century.

Franz's birth occurred just a few weeks after the move to the Seestrasse home. The two older sisters, Gertrude and Agathe, were ages three and four at the time. The architect for the new house was Emma's cousin, Herr Ernst Fiecher, who lived in Munich. Dr. Jung wrote him shortly after moving in, "Emma thinks much of her new house while she conceives Franz." Carl Jung also sent a telegram at the time of Franz's birth, dated November 27, 1908, to an unknown receiver: "Having dropped all my studies today because my wife is about to be confined, I at last have time to write to you." Later he writes: "Too bad we aren't peasants anymore, otherwise I could say, 'Now I have a son, I can depart in peace.'" This may be C. G.'s response to Freud's telegram of congratulation: "Special Good wishes to your little son, who is now embarking on psychic labors we still have no conception of. Franz Carl is thriving, I trust."

From a letter written by Carl Jung to Eugen Bleuler: "Everything is fine here. My wife, of course, is nursing the child herself, a pleasure for both of them. I feel that the conjunction of the birth of a son with a rationalization of the father complex is an extremely important turning point in my life, not least because I am now extricating myself from the social father-son relationship as well." It seems clear the father was examining his intended relationship with his new son, perhaps alongside his recollections of his own father.

CHAPTER SIX

CONSIDERING FRANZ

❁

IN THE INTERIM BEFORE OUR NEXT FACE-TO-FACE VISIT, WE HAD A fairly regular exchange of letters. Some of them were regarding my book *About Franz*, on which I worked in fits and starts. From our correspondence, I discovered Franz seemed to genuinely enjoy his life. He took great pleasure and pride in his own history as an architect of passion and considerable accomplishment. He was clearly a family man, devoted to his four sons and several grandchildren, a lively student of his side interests in anthropology and archeology, and he held a singular interest in the people who came to visit his family home during the final chapter of his life, to which I was fortunate to bear some witness. In his presence, one also became aware that he, the only son of Carl Jung, was surely the living male whom Dr. Jung knew and loved best in the world. Not an insignificant piece, that.

As I gathered the notes and memories of this story, I came to understood that Dr. Carl Jung plunged with observant attention and enormous courage into the human unconscious and drew from it the inner forms of the archetypes. But at the same time, he was constantly engaged in the process of making the inner forms visible in outer manifestations: in his mosaics, the multitude of small houses constructed with home-made mortar and sand, the Böllingen buildings, and in the powerful stone carvings, all of which manifested images of his inner world. We are now aware, from *The Red Book,* of his pleasure in creating small, thoughtful, and wondrous paintings. There was also the powerful drive to paint on walls.

Franz took part in many of the outward forms of Carl Jung's psyche. He began early on, first as a child collecting stones of the right color and size for the mosaics, then as partner in the building of the small towns on the seawall, then later as a young man aged fourteen as his father's helper in the building of the first tower at Böllingen, and still later as designer and advisor on the additions to the Böllingen complex.

He was his father's sensate comrade and, perhaps, a healthy balance for Carl Jung's powerful intuition. It was sensate Franz who consulted with his father as a young architect about paints that would last for the wall paintings at Bollingen. Franz assisted his father in finding the tools for the stone carvings. And it was Franz who came around whenever his father wanted help. Franz's own feelings about Bollingen were a mixture of respect and dismay, but he remained a staunch trustee of the Bollingen property, devoted to the principle that it must remain as his father designed it.

One could say that Carl Jung perfected the inner vision of the archetypes and also struggled to give them a tangible representation, while Franz took on a part of the manifestation of those outer forms, in a cooperative and thoroughly understandable, natural partnership. Yet Franz might find this idea of a natural partnership with his father to be a huge surprise. But one only has to visit some of Franz Jung's houses, or go to Bollingen, to imagine how this must have been.

•

Here, I must comment on an aspect of the Jungian analysis process as it relates to me. I was directed by my own analyst, Gary Hartman, that when you have a strong dream, it is a good thing to move the images into a different form. Of course, I write them down. But writing, for me, has always been a rather mundane art form. I played around with clay, but found it unresponsive, so for a while I painted my dreams in bright colors with poster paints. I was never very interested, even as a child, in painting images. Or so I thought. I still have one or two art books of my dreams from years ago, and I like to review them from time to time. They reflect an important period of my own personal progress.

But as I revisit my childhood memories, and even in later life, I recall I did love to play with coloring books and to paint pretty clothes for beautiful paper dolls as a teen-ager. At any rate, as I learned to deliver dream images to paper, I found it was in making the images that I finally learned to better understand each dream. Even the most superfluous details had meaning I would not have quite remembered otherwise. As I write this, I am struck with recalling how my mind stores music—songs, melodies, lyrics. There is always a tune going. Actually, if you ask me at most any moment of the day, "What is the song?" I could fish it out and deliver it to you without even needing to interrupt our conversation. I checked this out, this minute as I write, and the tune I am playing in my head, once I fish it out and bring it to my consciousness, seems to be an old Broadway song called "Anything Goes." Doesn't everyone do that, or something similar, all the time?

In my notes, I found the following:

It is true, Franz, before this return trip to visit you and Els, you were the story of C. G. Jung's interesting son. But now you are the warm, communicative, and delightful FRANZ, with a dear companion, ELS, and a rich and interesting inner life, some of which has been my great pleasure and privilege to hear, enjoy, and record. I can hardly thank you enough, Franz! Do you know?—

In friendship and deep gratitude, Mary Dian

I'm not sure this was sent, or if it was, I have no record of sending it. Another note to myself:

Like wooden hammers tapping a chisel on slate-like stone, there is a message for me to tap gently on the layered, slate-like stone of my own individuation process with a steady determination coupled with a more speculative, less judgmental, and perhaps more instinctive hand.

So has it been with this story.

•

During the times I was present in Küsnacht with Franz and/or Els, there were many walks. Franz liked his daily exercise and on several occasions invited me to accompany him when it was convenient or the weather permitted. As we walked, Franz would often point to one or another house and tell me the story of its occupants.

Here is a story that comes to mind: Franz was talking about his younger sister, Helene, the one closest to him in birth. He was telling me about the house he designed for her. He had a part in choosing the property and finally acquiring it for her, and then he told her how things should be arranged. Apparently he felt entitled to make the plans his way, and she, at one point, withdrew her invitation to have him design it since he constantly argued with her about how it should be done and what should go where. Franz laughed as he told the story and said he finally realized he had to let her participate in making the plans and be more agreeable about it, since it was, after all, going to be her house! This told to me with some humor on his part.

Another later time, as we were walking toward his younger sister's fine house, Franz told me the story of losing her in his later life and about all the work she was able to do for their father's work during her adult years. Whenever he talked about her, there was a lightness in his voice, and I learned she was a strong childhood friend as well as a close adult one, and he missed her. I later learned she was closely involved in the work *Kindertraume*, edited in part by Franz's son Lorenz.

My memory now goes tumbling back to other walks. One day we passed a lovely farm owned by a prosperous peasant family who stabled riding horses for people in Küsnacht and Zurich. Franz's granddaughter Christina was in high school and dearly loved horses and rode to exercise them after school at this farm. Alongside the turn in this conversation was the discussion of the word "peasant" and the differentiations necessary to describe the part of comparable American culture, which is so diverse that one word would not begin to describe the varieties of people in our culture that even come close to what is meant by "peasant" to a European.

Later, as we crossed a meadow, Franz spoke of his father as a deeply religious man, and he mentioned his own efforts, since his father's death, to learn as much as possible regarding this side of his father. He also told me about a letter he'd received from a group near Los Angeles wanting to visit Böllingen in May. He said he is often plagued with these sorts of requests and reserves his decision on whom he does or does not find suitable for such a visit. He led me to understand the criteria for his decision has to do with what sort of real familiarity the requesting people actually have with his father's work. He also mused on why a request from Peter Mudd of Chicago to see Böllingen had not come from Dr. Mudd, whom Franz knew from the Jung Institute.

On all our walks he spoke knowledgeably about the birds and plants in the area and Switzerland in general, a country small enough that everything managed by government is run quite efficiently, such as maintenance of the beautiful woodland where we walked. One day, lumbermen were busy hauling fallen trees and branches from recent storms, using horse-drawn sledges. Niko, Els's dog who came with us on our walks, was most excited by the horses and other dogs walking with their masters on the woodland paths.

On another day, we stopped to look at a rifle range and how the two ranges had been planned: one to accommodate large rifle practice and the second for smaller arms. Franz told me the name of the group that had commissioned this task and pointed out the advantages of the design for its intended purpose to help me better understand the process involved. In the telling, it seemed to carry him back to his military service. I mentioned my father had taught me how to fire an Italian Beretta, a trophy of his from World War II. Franz told me a story of when he had been on border patrol in the Alps and about his experience with Italian soldiers. He said that while all fraternization of any kind was prohibited, there had been an exchange of cigarettes, food, and conversation, and he had also acquired a small Beretta, "Nice, but inaccurate," he said.

I told him my story of walking into the Georgia woods as a young woman with my father at Christmas time when my father, carrying a rifle, would shoot down mistletoe growing high in the stately old trees because mistletoe is a favorite plant to bring inside at Christmas. Franz was most interested in this custom, having never heard of such a practice as well as the tradition of kissing a girl standing under the mistletoe. He laughed as he heard my story and said it was a very fine custom.

During another walk, there was a view of a lovely farm from where we were standing at a higher place. It spread before us in the sunlight, a handsome spread of buildings, fields, and grazing animals. He knew the people who owned the farm and remarked, "They have done very well," meaning that the farm was prosperous. We walked in the Walde, west of the Tobel, and I saw a white horse grazing in one of the pastures, and a golden retriever. Immediately, an old nursery song came into my mind: "Ride a cock horse to Banbury Cross to see a fine lady upon a white horse. Rings on her fingers and bells on her toes, she shall have music wherever she goes."

Another story had to do with their grandmother. When they were young children, he and his sister walked to school together and passed Grandmother's house on the way to and fro. Grandmother usually had treats of some sort, and they always felt welcome. However, Grandmother had a sense of discomfort in her house. She sensed there were invasive spirits that came in whenever the doors were opened. At night, she was known to glue small pieces of white paper on each door that opened to the outside world. If, in the morning, any of her papers were torn or loosened, she would assume the doors had been opened, letting spirits come into the house, and she would charge from room to room, flipping a towel to shoo them out again. Young Franz and his sister were delighted to view this phenomena.

When Franz told this tale to me, I recalled reading in one of the books on Jung family history that when Great-Grandfather, who was a Protestant theologian, sat in the dining room on Saturday evenings to write his sermon for the following morning, his little daughter was assigned the task of using a towel to shoo away any evil spirits behind him while he worked. And that was the little girl who grew up to be Grandmother still shooing away the evil spirits! Later, Franz shared a story, which I shall retell here as best I can: "About the time when my mother Emma died, in 1955, my father suffered a period of depression that seemed to last a long time. I shopped around and found a good stone for carving and had it delivered to the house. It didn't challenge my father for a while, but soon I heard the tap-tap of chisel on stone and knew my father was somewhat recovering." This was the large stone that sat in the Seestrasse garden.

It was Franz's sensate skill and his loving sense of his father's needs that must have provided Carl with many hours of relief, exercise, and the silent demands of time and patience necessary for the artist in him, alongside the gifted scientist and practicing psychiatrist, to survive his lifetime and make way for the creation of so many true art works that may well last for hundreds of years.

Dear Franz,   *March 22, 1989*

I must tell you again how very much I enjoyed my time in Küsnacht and how deeply I appreciate every kindness you have extended in my behalf. It was an extraordinary experience for me. And on some level, I also believe it has been good for you as well.

I deeply appreciated your corrections, opinions, and suggestions for my preliminary manuscript, all of which were helpful. Prior to this discussion, I was unclear regarding just what I wanted to write for publication. But now I feel that whatever the manuscript contains, it is primarily about you—your life in the early years with your father and family; your work as an architect of conviction and principle; your position in the world as a scholarly, educated man whose accomplishments have rewarded you; and the role you have assumed now, in your retirement years, of devotion to your father's life and accomplishments and service to your family. It was important for me to see your work not as merely an extension of your father, but as a task for you after fulfilling your own career. It was very important for me to understand this part, and you made every effort, as the weeks progressed, to see to it that I had an experiential opportunity to explore and enjoy an exposure to the real Franz Jung's interests and environment.

Also, through the natural grace of your warm personality, I was given the opportunity to see the Böllingen retreat through your eyes with the gentle help of your friend Els Glasser. Once again, I returned from a visit with you to make copious notes, not only of the powerful energy of the place, but of your obvious pleasure and enthusiasm in conducting me. I saw the towers as they are, not only as a famous shrine for other Jungian pilgrims, but also as a place where men, particularly, are drawn to experiencing the exhilarating task of pitting human strength alongside that of nature. Here there is both solitude and triumph, and a metaphor of what human beings must do alongside nature itself and thereby learn something of their own inner nature.

In a sense, whatever else there is, there is always a Böllingen place to be made, chiseled from the brain stem through the body into sheer rock, itself. Böllingen says, for both you and your father: NEVERTHELESS, I AM. So it was, also, for Folsom Man and his blade, for the Ashanti and the caves of Mesa Verde. As science and technology move relentlessly into the silicon cells of the very heart of the computer and microcomputer, we move in thought out to the antennae of satellites spinning in space that connect your world and mine in a new immediacy. In both directions, man chisels away. And for you, Franz, this also exists in the many houses of your design and in the hearts and minds of your rapidly growing family.

Of all your many answers to my ubiquitous questions, I am strangely fascinated by the notion of the small wooden hammer necessary for the chisel to carve the stone. Perhaps it is a metaphor for me to tap gently on the rocks and stones of my own process with both determination and flexibility, along with my memories of Franz and Els.

I am also confronted with the image of the great twelve-pointed star mandala on the wall by the closet in the tower. I have tried to make a few preliminary drawings and must carry it on. That one is quintessence. As I left the room, I recall softly patting the bed, as a sort of "thank you" to C. G. Jung.

I shall not forget how you moved ahead of me at Böllingen that first time, upstairs, downstairs, in, out, opening the windows for light, and leading us with your great keys. And whether you are comfortable with the idea or not, I must tell you, once again, that this is exactly the way a woman's well-developed animus works on the internal level of psyche. So I must tell you, my friend, that which you provided for me in a concretized external version, for one day in time, was a totally internal process for me. And if my own internal animus continues to treat me nearly as well as you did, with care, consideration, grace, and respect, then I am also more able to do the same for myself and my work. There is some sense, for me, of entitlement, that somehow you believed I was entitled to have this splendid experience. And so I must also believe it. I closed the gate at Böllingen, as you know, with a heart like an open sponge, my eyes flowing, barely able to talk. At the fine dinner with Els at her house, we were all our most comfortable, natural selves, just people of the world enjoying mutual interests, conversation, delicious food, and the pleasure of each other's company and companionship. There was a relaxed creative sharing of those things that enrich our lives in such different parts of the world. I can hardly thank you enough.

In friendship, Mary Dian

P.S. I shall also remember what you said to me that evening about this idea of writing about you for possible publication: "I am a complicated man, and you barely know me. If you should seek to look further, then we shall see. The project moves as it can. There is no other way." As I told you, I will not submit for publication anything concerning you that does not meet with your consensus. So if you can endure, another manuscript will be forthcoming. I had a dream of you last evening in which you clearly told me, "There are four ways of being present." I took this as a reminder, from my own subconscious, that the perception of my experience with you, as I write, must include all four of the functions: thinking, feeling, intuition, and sensate functions. Since I am a so-called "extroverted intuitive thinker," I might need to screen my piece for adequate representation of the feeling and sensate worlds. If I am correct, it is Els, and you as well that carry, superbly, the feeling function.

I do pretty well intuiting the feelings of others, but I rarely know, exactly, what are my own! So I would want her to assist us in whatever editing might be ahead, if you approve. Combined with your splendid sensate function, all bases should be adequately covered. Perhaps we can, with the help of you both, come up with a piece that even C. G. himself might have approved. It won't be world-shaking, but I think it might be worthwhile. After all, you well deserve some public recognition for your splendid work, your distinguished record, and your truly warm heart.

The following is Franz's letter in reply.

Dear Mary Dian,   August 20, 1989

Time has passed since your very nice visit. Els and I are still enjoying our talks in Küsnacht and more recently your long letters, which I am sorry have to be answered in my handwriting, and I hope you have not too much difficulty to decipher it. If someone were to make a critique of my work, they must first look at the plans. I was very careful about the smallest detail of moldings and woodwork and prepared desks and tables and wide comfortable beds. I made a cradle on wheels and liked to design from the basic concepts of style from earlier times, but with every possible convenience. I was a stickler for every possible detail.

There were ten houses in Küsnacht, a few in Baden, Zurich, all in Switzerland. Assisted with one near Florence, kitchens, particularly.

People still compliment me on the comfort, particularly, and the convenience of my houses. I also designed a Catholic Church while in a Catholic regiment, but I didn't get to build it.

Now for our "business" about my interest in American prehistoric times. I thank you very much for taking my interests in earnest and sending the list of books on archeology that might interest me. In reality it is not so urgent or important. So do not try to trace half of American archaeologists to run after the Folsom points, which are actually just one of my tiny little dots of a very vast field absolutely unknown to me, as I read last fall something of these Folsom points. It is just that name that keeps in my memory. In reality, my interest lies more on a general level: How come it is that a huge continent has lost nearly all facts of early populations? As far as I know, one has today the theory that the population of America (North and South) has come from Alaska or Siberia in a time when Bering (Bering?) Straights was still land. It seems to be a fact that Asiatic and Eskimo people have wandered down south during thousands of years. Surely they must have left some traces of the last 700,000–500,000 years as we find them in Europe, Africa, and Asia. In all these countries, the last 100 years have brought to light a rich material in bone and stone tools, besides parts of human skeletons to have archaeologists show a line of development which begins earlier than one million years and can be followed down to our present time. I am sure, something similar can or already has been found in USA, at least in places that had never been covered in that time.

Prior to Folsom seems to be Clovis Complex, and certainly much older paleo-Indian complexes, and not only in the southwest.

For my more general interest, a book as mentioned under B or C, (Bryan, New evidence for Pleistocene/Revins or Ericson, Taylor-Burger, Peopling the New World) would be very interesting. If ever you could get such a book, please send me a copy of the chapter or a summary, so I could judge it. But please do not haste, it has all its time. Many thanks for your help. As you wrote in your letter to Els, the book C. G. Jung: Word and Image can't be found in Kansas City. It came out in 1979 in Princeton, New Jersey, 08540. You could ask for the series of Böllingen Books, series xx. Let me close my letter with best greetings from Els, who is talking of a Tele-party with Kansas spices. She certainly will write you one of these days, and from me my best compliments.

Franz

This was followed shortly thereafter by a letter from Els.

Dear Mary Dian:

Your big parcel with the most interesting American spices has arrived, just the day before we left for our holiday in the mountains. I had just the time to open it, and I must say that you are really spoiling us, and Franz and I thank you very much for the wonderful bar-b-que set which I know I will enjoy trying. What a pity you cannot join us when we celebrate our first bar-b-que party!

Franz and I, we both enjoy our holiday in the mountains very much. We have wonderful weather and can go skiing every day.

I hope you are well and happy. I remember our fine time together with pleasure. I am looking forward to hearing from you and send you all my best wishes.

Els

Dear Els,

It was a pleasure to hear from you and to learn you had a fine skiing vacation. This is one activity which so many people enjoy. I grew up where there were nice hills but few mountains, and I never was a very good athlete. So I've decided to leave skiing for my next life, along with singing at the Metropolitan Opera, scuba-diving, and cooking with a Chinese wok! I know it is wonderful exercise, and you and Franz make excellent advocates for cross-country since you are both so fit. I am delighted to have the pictures were made at your home. I have looked at them long and hard, trying to recall details of the room, particularly the little landscape oil painting over the shot of you and Franz . . . such a beautiful sky! I would like to walk the country lane leading to the white speck of a farmhouse in the distance. And in the shots of me and Franz, we look very intent on our conversation, while the white cow in the painting keeps an eye on things. Is there a shepherd lying in the foreground, head propped in hand? And a collie dog? Is this perhaps an English landscape or French, perhaps? I'd like so much to know! Els, I also recall the book, I think the title was *Word and Image*, which Franz said was published by Böllingen Press. He said there is an English version. I thought perhaps Warren, my husband, had purchased it as he misses very few Jung books, but no, it is not anywhere in Kansas City, so I must order it. If it is not too much trouble, I'd love to check the English title with you. It is the book with all the splendid pictures.

And the photograph of the Böllingen Tower, which you gave me, is a great treasure. And I keep my little stone, which I picked up by the lakeside, on the table beside me in my office so that when there are stressful moments doing therapy, I hold it in my hand, and all things grow very quiet inside. I am sure you understand this!

Keep in touch.

Fondly, Mary Dian

I was thoroughly charmed by her letter and thought of her as a fine companion to Franz. In the meantime, my life, as usual, was full and the time slipped away from me. Finally, in late October, I answered Franz's previous letter.

Dear Franz,   October 30, 1989

I am embarrassed to have been so long silent and to have failed to send you a second manuscript. But now I can send an explanation and am ready to begin once more on my project. I do hope you have had a pleasant, healthy summer.

The last time we spoke by telephone, you sounded hearty and busy as you were expecting some interesting visitors. I am particularly interested to hear how you reacted to Giles Quispell, whom I met in 1988 at the Institute.

I have begun to plan another trip to Küsnacht in early 1990, if it is possible to visit with you then. My head is full of things I would like to discuss with you, and I only hope it is not an imposition to intrude upon your busy life once again. In order to discuss this with you, I shall plan to call you on November 21st at about 7:00 P.M. your time. If this is inconvenient or you are planning to be out of town, do let me know, and we can set another time. The manuscript will be in the mail to you by January 1st, I do believe!

Please give my warm best wishes to dear Els and tell her I hope to see her in 1990!

Cordially, Mary Dian

P.S. My little Böllingen stone was lost for part of the summer, and yesterday, as I was reading Barbara Hanna's book, I knew suddenly that the stone must be under the credenza in my office! Sure enough, it was. My cat had rolled it off my desk. I am so glad to have it back in place, and I am certain that its reclamation has enabled me to write to you once again and pick up where we were!

In retrospect, Franz carried in his presence a commitment to a very singular, very specific mode of hospitality that respects the history and tradition of the family and indeed something of the spiritual essence of his father and his place in the world order. But in no way was Franz Jung a mere tour guide of his father's intimate surroundings. He was, instead, a man who managed to be cordially apart from the world of psychological inquiry while still maintaining a healthy respect for his father's work and a lively interest in the people who associate themselves with the Jungian world. Something of his own poise in this effort seemed to have been a rather remarkable achievement of selfhood. He was both engrossed in his father's story and somehow also quite free of it, a man involved, yet quite comfortably apart.

CHAPTER SEVEN

My Return

✳

Dear Franz,   January 6, 1990

Thank you for your letter of November 30th. It arrived here on December 19th, at which time I framed a response to you, but the activities of the holidays carried me off and only this week has life settled down to a more reasonable routine.

I am indeed grateful to Els for offering me a room in her home and look forward to that arrangement enormously. And while it is possible that I may need to visit with a few people in Zurich, I am coming principally to talk with you and Els about the material I hope to write and upon which we have already begun, regarding you and your life.

I promised a second manuscript to be in the post by the New Year, but once again there have been unavoidable delays. At this juncture, the piece is in the hands of my typist, and I expect a mailing date soon. I am realizing now that the delay in my schedule which requires me to come at a later date will be very helpful in order to fulfill some standing responsibilities and projects here, and I only hope this will be comfortable for you and Els as well. In order to answer your question of what it is I want, I will tell you. Ever since our first meeting, I have been intrigued with your position in your father's life, and I want to write about that. How to approach the subject, or from what premise, has only recently become more clear to me as I read more about architecture and learn more about you—as a boy, with your father, and the ways in which you assisted him in making visual representations of his world.

There were numerous ways in which you assisted him to make visual, tactile stones for the early mosaics, the building of the village on the sea wall, the early building of the Böllingen tower in 1923, and the later development of the upper story in 1955. As I understand it, you were deeply involved in his process of creativity, or that part which existed outside his practice and writing, which made visual representations of his inner world. Also, your present role as the owner and senior inhabitant and curator of the family home and work place suggests the ongoing function of your part in his life.

While the full essence of the relationship which existed between you and your father may never be fully grasped, something in it, I believe, assisted him in very tangible ways.

He needed a human being to join him in building and caring for the structures that were tangibly important to him, and you were that person. The impact of his need upon you must have influenced the direction of your path as well. He loved you more, I imagine, than any other male figure in his life, and he trusted you as both child and adult to help him. But the book I want to write is as much about Franz and the archetypal process of architecture as it is about C. G. I am not sure how this will all develop, or even if, since I'm not sure you will agree to let me pursue this further. My intention now is to proceed more as a journalist, seeking facts rather than a contriver of any vast thesis I might manipulate to prove. I do know the size and the scope of the book which I hope to write must be determined by the degree to which we remain comfortable together in this dialogue. I am sure you must have asked yourself just why I have remained so attentive, Franz. The truth is that I am very much drawn to this task and to your story. There is an internal energy in it for me, and each time I let it float away, I am given another dream indicating that you, I, and Els have work to do together.

Perhaps what you can do best for me before my visit is to explore how you feel about this undertaking. Truthfully, I expect you to resist the task because you are a modest person. Basically, I am coming this time for three reasons:

1. To seek your permission and help to write a book about you;

2. To review what notes I have and develop some new ones, if you agree; and

3. If the above are agreed upon, to develop a suitable plan and outline.

I must also tell you that I see Els as an essential enabler of the project, without whose presence in your life this would not be possible. Just as you brought us together at Böllingen so that we might all three learn to be comfortable together, so is she now, with her lovely understanding of you, a most necessary and important part of this task, for me.

I would like to share with you and Els the three dreams which have visited me about you and this project. I consider them to be an important challenge from my unconscious and one to which I must remain attentive, and to you both and this project. I have taken them to my private analyst, Gary Hartman, to seek his interpretation as well. I have also considered that it is possible you have come to an agreement with some other writer about this project regarding your biographical material. If this is so, I will of course withdraw from this plan entirely. I only hope this is not the case. Also, should this be agreeable to you, I have a great interest in seeing, and possibly photographing, any other buildings of your design that you would care to share with me, and any information you may have about Ernst Feicher of Munich whom I understand to have been the architect of the Seestrasse house.

I look forward to talking with you a week from now, on January 15th, and will send this letter off to you by special delivery in hope that you will have read it by then.

Best wishes, Mary Dian

Dear Mary Dian   February 15, 1990

Thank you so very much for your call, announcing your visit to Küsnacht for April 1990. I asked Els Glasser if she could let you have her spare room. She is happy if you could accept her room, which is very suitable, and no bathroom adjacent, but it would make things much more practical and she and we can see you as much as time allows. I do not know exactly the reason of your coming, I would be glad if you could write me occasionally to tell me the purpose so I can prepare myself a bit in advance. Even if you came to Zurich at quite another night, your staying at Frau Glasser's room is by no means for you an obligation to reserve your time for us! You are certainly absolutely free to do what you want. But we both welcome and are happy to see you here, even if your time is also for other people.

I had a busy week with invitations, both active and passive, *some boring, some nice, birthday celebration (my own!), burials, memorials, etc. I am glad to return about next week to a normal way of life! I hope you and your husband had a good Christmas and look forward to your answer,*

Kindest regards, Franz

Shortly after receiving the letter from Franz, Els Glasser wrote to me.

Dear Mrs. Molton,   *February 20, 1990*

Franz Jung just told me you are definitely coming to visit in April and we are both looking forward with pleasure to seeing you again, and I am so happy to welcome you as my guest in my home! We certainly will have a good time together. Franz and I, we both insist to come to the airport. If you don't take the flight SR #15 as mentioned, but have a chance to get a seat on another flight via American Airlines, please cable before stating the flight number and the arrival time; otherwise we shall be at the station at 10:15 on Sunday, April 1st. We are leaving for our skiing vacation next Saturday and return on March 6th, so we are certainly fit when you arrive. With all our pleasure to see you soon, we remain with our best regards.

Cordially Yours, Els Glasser

P.S. Please forgive me for not having written to you before this and answered to your nice letter. In my thoughts I wrote to you many times, but my bad English stopped me to do it in reality!

On April 2, 1990, I once more arrived in Zurich on Swiss Air. The wait to go through customs was long and tedious, so I suggested to Els that I travel into Küsnacht via the train. She would have none of it, and so she and Franz were waiting for me when I reached the end of the customs line. We drove to Küsnacht. They could both sense how tired I was after my long flight, and so we went directly to Els's house. As Franz bid me goodbye, he said we, meaning Els and I, should come to his house for lunch the next day. I don't remember nodding, but I'm sure I did.

Els fixed me a snack, and I settled my things in the nice little room which she uses for an office/study at Obere Heslibach Str. #79, just across the way from the house where Franz and Lilly raised their boys. I took a nap, being very tired, and Franz came over at perhaps 3:30 or so. I called Toni Baker and made plans to see him Monday at 5:45 P.M. I also called my friends Elton and Ella Squires, and made plans for us to meet on Tuesday for dinner at Chez Falcon.

In the morning, Els and I had some quiet reading time before we joined Franz around noon. I again noticed the painting of a man astride a beautiful white horse and was again thrilled to be in this house—my third time to climb those elegant stairs—and the mystery and excitement of my earlier visits swept through me. I consciously made an effort to move carefully, all antennae out. Franz was busy in the kitchen, slicing sausages into a fragrant onion sauce. Els made a quick trip back to her home to fetch her camera. Franz and I went into the library to wait and sat together on the sofa. While she was gone, Franz explained that on the floor above this one are five sleeping rooms used by his son Andreas and his family, one of which Andreas uses for his private work room. Over the garage, there are living quarters for the Hispanic man and his wife who are the gardeners for the grounds. Franz laughed as he told me the man had very specific ideas on woman's work. For example, when the fruit trees are ready to be picked, the man leans the ladder against a tree and calls his wife to climb up, carefully pick the fruit, and toss it down, one by one.

Els soon arrived and took a photo of the two of us sitting on the sofa. Soon, our dinner was underway: fine sausages, potatoes, apple sauce, carrot salad and a green salad, white wine, ice cream, coffee, and biscuits, plus a splendid Swiss chocolate. Franz called his kitchen a "creative confusion." But in truth, there was little confusion.

During the meal, at one point, Els and Franz dropped their careful English and lapsed into rapid German. They then looked at me sheepishly, "Sorry."

After this fine meal, Els and Franz tidied up. A tender, teasing moment occurred when Els told Franz to be careful of the delicate wine glasses as he replaced them high in the cupboard. He touched the tip of her nose with his finger, gave her a little kiss, and said "I know quite well how to handle delicate things." Soon, Els left us to our work and drove off, but not before reminding Franz of their evening dinner schedule. Before we began to talk, I had a fleeting moment upon entering the library door that Franz's father was here in the room with us, sitting in the library chair by the window at the other end of the room, perhaps reading.

I mentioned this sensing to Franz. He began speaking of Lilly and Emma as being "here in the house with me from time to time; they comfort me," he said quickly. He went on to tell me of the death of his friend's wife and seemed morose. "Death is such a common part of life," he added. Our conversation then veered to a local barn somewhere in the area where tile are reported to fly in some sort of telekinesis. A young girl, they say, is known to be present. For some reason, I think of incidents in *Memories, Dreams, Reflections,* Carl Jung's memoir, of similar experiences and recall also that his sister Gertrude might have been present for those events, as well. The pairing of young girls with stories of this nature has remained in my mind.

We began our work with corrections on my earlier manuscript, and Franz told me the story of his purchase of the Seestrasse house, following his father's death in 1961, when he, Lilly, and their sons moved in. Lilly was, at that time, working on the editing of *The Collected Works of C. G. Jung,* and the boys were fairly mature and in their twenties. Christof and his wife, Christina, moved into Franz and Lilly's previous house where they were still living and where Christof conducted his architectural company.

Franz picked up his portfolio of correspondence and mused through some letters. "This correspondence takes up many of my hours," he said.

I smiled and suggested his informal role as curator of the private library, host to visitors from all over the world, and correspondence, has become, indeed, his second career. He selected a few letters to share, one asking for help from a man who was an Inspector General of Police from Islamabad and wanted to study at the Institute. Another concerned Meier's work on the Pauli manuscripts. Franz said Meier's work on "what is a thought" is remarkable. Another letter was from a man who wanted Franz to answer two questions: 1) What is the exact nature of C. G's. relationship to Toni Wolf? and 2) What is the nature of Jung's Christian faith? Franz was annoyed about the latter since it was obvious the writer had an agenda of his own. The man had chosen to omit any mention of his own Jungian studies. "If indeed, there were any," Franz said. He had, however, written a polite letter, referring the writer to previously published biographies. Franz was always a gentleman. We launched into a conversation on the subject of the complementarity of reason and intuition and moved into Jung's notion of complementarity in psychology. Franz liked to discuss the threads of his father's work that interested him particularly over the years. He also mentioned Marie-Louis von Franz's work, *Psyche and Matter,* and gave me the name of Bob Henshaw to secure a copy. I was once again struck by the impressive knowledge Franz had on what has been written in the Jungian corpus, as well as the seemingly faultless recall he has of the biographical data of his father's life.

"There were many letters in the household," he said. "Unfortunately, they were apt to be rather casually handled at times. Or even used to light the fires!"

He then told me of his trip to London, carrying Freud's letters to Jung in a suitcase to meet with Ernst Freud. The Freud archives have had a professional curator, Mr. Patterson, for many years. But up until the time Frau Aniela Jaffe became Jung's official secretary, much of what went on at his father's desk was managed by whatever available help was at hand, and often things fell by the wayside. Franz mentioned a letter from Ferenczi, the Hungarian psychoanalyst, to Freud that might shed light on this topic. Linda Donn, in her study of Freud and Jung, had found an old family retainer of the Freud family in Vienna and learned much from her, including information on the letter from Ferenczi.

As the shadows of evening began to drift through the room, Franz spoke of Carl Jung and Emma. "Their presence is with me here," he said, "and it comforts me." For a fleeting moment, I saw Carl Jung at his desk in the corner, across the room, watching us. I shook my head to clear it . . . the floor creaked. Franz quietly said, "For me, death is so much a part of life." As we finished our talk in the library, Els arrived for their dinner engagement and took a picture of Franz and me, sitting. I am on the couch and Franz in the chair, facing me and all our papers. I gathered up my papers and prepared to leave.

"Thank you for today," I said. "Have a lovely time with Els this evening, and we will see each other tomorrow."

"We shall go for a walk," Franz said and bowed a courtly nod as he held my hand. "I should also like you to tell me why you have chosen to write about your visits with me and how well you know your own unconscious." I told him I would think over his request and respond as truthfully as I possibly could.

As I walked back under the streetlights, I thought about what he had told me of his trip to visit Ernst Freud. I wondered if that was a defining moment for Franz as he moved into the dignity of being the arbiter of his father's world and publications and the world of interested readers of his father's life. He took some pleasure and enormous sense of responsibility for that. But he had also become a spokesman for his family. Yes, he was an architect but also a man who had taken on a great responsibility. It would be many years before I saw the published volume of Freud / Jung letters.

At one time later when we were talking, I asked Franz if I had seen his father's meditation room when we were at Böllingen. I recalled we were walking along a hallway, and Franz had mentioned "meditation room" as we passed quickly by a closed door as if to imply that this was not for public attention. I said that if so, I had no memory of it, and he nodded his head, implying that this remains a closed room. In retrospect, I do not believe this room has ever been publicly seen or described in print or perhaps even entered. If so, I have never read any description nor heard about the contents, paintings, or memorabilia.

This information seems to have been a well-kept secret among the family members. I remember Franz mentioned the *geheimnis* (secret) about Böllingen, which he casually said to me once but waved away when I questioned him about the word.

In the morning, I was out early and ready for breakfast at the Ochsen Café. I needed to exchange some travelers' checks but banks didn't open until 8:30. So after thoroughly enjoying my *kline frushtick*, complete with much butter and fabulous bread, I headed into Zurich on the train. I managed the trip a little less efficiently than I had expected since there had been a change since my last visit to Stadelhoffen station, but I found my way and had a second round of coffee at the Stadelhoffen restaurant while waiting for the bank to open. After cashing my travelers' checks, I went to see Toni Baker, my analyst. When one is studying at the Jungian Institute, it is customary to have an analyst, and she had been very supportive of my wanting to write about Franz Jung. My time with Toni was spent exploring as deeply as possible what my motives were in my trip, what I had discovered, and what I hoped to discover. It was a delight for me to find my responses understood and validated. By 11:30, I was back in Els's apartment, and we scurried off to buy our groceries for the evening party as the stores close from noon to 1:30 P.M., and I wanted to be prepared to accompany Franz on our afternoon walk.

So off we went to the market!

I was principal cook, preparing two dishes totally unknown to Els, in her kitchen, which made shopping complicated. I could hardly make myself understood as to what groceries I needed and had to explain, in English, what kind of sausages I wanted so Els could translate my needs into German. But we managed! I'd brought rice and seasonings from home for the jambalaya, which helped some. And for the bananas foster, bananas and ice cream were available in the store and needed no translating. Dinner was scheduled for 7:00 P.M. I knew I needed about three hours in the kitchen for cooking, which meant this day would be more carefully scheduled than others, yet very interesting in how it had come about. A friend of mine was also at the Institute along with his wife. My friendship with Elton and Ella Squires went back several years, and so I had asked if I could invite them. Franz and Els were both gracious in their response, and I was pleased to be able to introduce them. And so our dinner party would consist of five people.

We had great fun setting the table with Els's elegant pink linen tablecloth and handsome folded napkins, placing the shining silver and sparkling crystal at each place. It was as if we had done this together many times. Something like a sisterhood was formed over this evening meal, reflecting the few days we had shared and the fun of having such a sense of compatibility right from the start!

I really do like to cook for the people I'm fond of. And I've learned how to concentrate fully upon the preparation of food so it comes out exactly as I wish for those who are gathered. It is a gift to and from my own sensate function.

After we decided to invite Elton and Ella for this Cajun feast, we also had many conversations on whether the jambalaya would be palatable to Franz. He preferred foods mildly seasoned, and as I had learned more about his eating tastes during this trip, I became less sure he would enjoy it. But it was decided among us that we would hold some bread, cheese, and ham in reserve if the dish wasn't to Franz's taste and proceeded with the menu.

Els said, "It does not matter if you do or do not like it, Franz. What matters is that Mary Dian prepares it and her friends enjoy it." The question of dessert arose. My family is very fond of bananas foster with a lovely hot rum sauce with fruit served over ice cream. Since it is a New Orleans specialty, I had suggested this one and had brought the recipe with me from home. But it involved last minute preparation, so there would be a kitchen scurry to serve it. With a flambé, no less!

I had taken on a flambéed dessert in the kitchen of a woman with whom I had experienced only the beginnings of a friendship. However, I knew, by instinct, it would all work out because Els and I seemed to understand each other quickly and well, step by step as our friendship had grown. Nevertheless, there was a small anxiety in me—the complex of one who fears being "too muchness" in a country other than home.

Before the guests arrived, Els and I stirred the fragrant pot of jambalaya and tended the rice amid clattering pots and pans. At one point, we met each other in the middle of the kitchen floor and danced around for a minute together and hugged each other like school girls having a party. My whispering complex gave me brief scenes of fantasy: Franz politely toying with a food he could not bear; Els's entire kitchen in flames, the lovely apartment reduced to cinders. Something inside—my better voice—shushed my fears and told me not to be so silly. All would be fine.

Els set out a lovely lunch of salmon, capers, onions, bread, and butter and wanted me to enjoy it. Franz arrived at 3:30 ready to walk. Els sent us off with her dog, Nico, and we rode by car up the hill past Welti's winery and onto a different set of paths. We talked of migratory birds and fish, he sharing his vast information of the many colored finches, stories of the salmon's travels up and down the river, and the swallows nesting in his boathouse with access under the small swooping eaves and their return every year. "How do they know to come back to Franz Jung's boathouse each year?" Franz said and shook his head. "They just do. Lilly enjoyed them, so I carried a chase lounge out on the balcony so she could watch. She smiled, certain she recognized the ones from previous years."

He pointed out the rifle range some distance away, which we had passed on an earlier walk. And for some reason, he added, "We still have two full days to work."

I understood he meant he was not ready to resume yesterday's conversation, and that it pleased him to speak in conversation that occurred to him in the small voices of nature. As some Swiss military B35 fighter planes flew overhead, he talked of the Swiss military, and the questions and problems of atomic power.

A silence fell between us for a few moments. We continued walking. I finally bolstered my courage. "May I tell you a dream I had recently?" He looked amused but nodded. "I dreamed I was with a group of adults, standing outside the entrance to the first tower, waiting to be admitted. A little girl, perhaps no more than four or five years old, was dancing around, in and out, among the guests, very excited about being there." I wondered who she was, and after I told this story, Franz shook his head and smiled. "The *geheimness*, perhaps," meaning "secret." He stood up and looked around for his coffee cup.

Ah, the *geheimness*...my very own internal little girl who still remains excited about the entire Böllingen thing. Secret? I ask myself. Or perhaps she is my own little-girl excitement, still, about delivering this story. I like to think also of the "secret" of what I thought about "Aimalee's Star." It was in 2019, perhaps, when I discovered "Aimalee" must have been Carl Jung's mother, Emilie. My own fantasy was that Carl Jung painted the star in honor of Emilie's spiritual nature, and formed, in Carl Jung, a mental system that acknowledged, identified, and honored, the presence of distinctly spiritual mysteries as a primal archetypal construct in the human race. Of the fantasies described somewhere in Jung's early descriptions of the property up at Böllingen when he first bought the land just three months after his mother's death, there still remains a mystery.

It has taken me many years to make those connections and move them into my own consciousness. And to take this one step further, it brings into consciousness the positive tone that repeats, "I don't believe. I know." This concept has influenced my own life and, one by one over the years, that of my family and many of my clients.

I can only re-create, in simplistic terms, how that worked for me over the years when I had to reframe the God concept beyond the religion model in which I was raised as a child to a much broader vision. And if that archetype is present to all of us, one way or another, it is quite possible that it lives in us in many image forms: Art? Music? Food? Poetry? Intellectual life? Astrology? Family life? Psychotherapy? God? Love? The list could go on and on.

It is certain to me that each of these has entered my office at one time or another and is given the divine, omnipresence in life that actually belongs to "other than human" priority and power. Do they change periodically? Sometimes. Yes. But each time they may become "larger than life," as we so freely say, in one's own *geheimness* place. Whatever that is, it occupies the religion or God archetypal place. Omnipresent, in one form or another, either positively or negatively charged, in our minds. Emilie was the same grandmother Franz spoke of with such enthusiasm for her association with the naughty "spirits" that seemed such a part of her entire life, beginning with flipping a towel around her father's sermon writing on Saturday evenings. Later on, I thought of the childlike excitement I'd felt, going to Bòllingen, and later, wanting to write about it. The child in the dream might have been my own childlike feminine excitement, both for the day itself and the thought of writing the story of Franz. *Geheimness*: secret, mystery.

We returned to Els's apartment an hour later. Franz was in no hurry to leave. Els had prepared the table for the evening party, the rose-colored tablecloth now beautifully appointed with rose-colored napkins and glistening silver and china. Franz exclaimed, as did I, how handsome the table looked. I said, "Franz, I must go to the kitchen pots if there is to be a party." He laughed and said, "And I must go and dress appropriately for it!" I set about finishing the jambalaya as Els prepared a green salad while also observing what I was making. "I enjoy watching you do this. You manage it with an accustomed confidence," she said. I remember thinking that Els is a remarkable wise woman, full of spirited playfulness and warmth. This trusting and lovely bond remained between us as we gave a party together. What a natural, pleasant way for women to become close friends. None of the austere reserve I had known from some other Swiss women inhibited Els's fun-loving spirit or deterred us from enjoying each other. By 7:00, the house was full of the Cajun fragrance, the meal ready, the hostesses dressed, and Franz returned, dressed in coat and tie, rested and in good spirits. "The fragrance of your dish greeted me all the way outside!" he said.

Elton and Ella Squires arrived, bearing a gorgeous bouquet of white tulips, and the evening was underway. Els had prepared a little pastry aperitif, which we enjoyed at the coffee table, the white tulips resplendent in a lovely vase in the center. Franz was taken with Ella, a glowing, beautiful young American from Louisiana, and a math teacher by profession. However, she was unable to secure a job teaching in Switzerland and so secured a position as a mail carrier for the Küsnacht Post Office in order to assist with the finances to see Elton through his training at the Jung Institute. Franz considered this a remarkable feat and wanted to know how she managed the appointment. He laughed and said, "I think you must have had to petition all the way to Bern for such a job!" We moved to the table for dinner, and the conversation continued along pleasantly. Franz poured an excellent burgundy from one of those nice little Italian basket holders and helped himself to a second and healthy portion of my spicy Cajun dish.

He began a story of the founding of Friends of Jung in Louisiana. He had met a very short woman who had come to Küsnacht with her tall, beautiful daughter. Franz was particularly amused by the contrast of the tall, beautiful dark-eyed daughter and the short, stocky mother. The woman had learned that Carl Jung had once visited Louisiana and stayed at a sort of lumber farm somewhere south of New Orleans, and so, on her return, she arranged a large party with many guests, 200 or so, at this lumber farm, including people from the psychological community of Louisiana. On the night of this party the Friends of Jung in Louisiana was established with many members. Nearly everyone present signed up!

The bananas foster with which we ended the meal turned out splendidly, except the flambé refused to catch fire properly, but the sauce was great on the pan-seared bananas and ice cream. We ended the meal, laughing over Kafee Hag, a decaf, instant coffee, which our guests requested and Els produced. Contrary to her usual precise standards, she lightheartedly spooned the decaf into cups and added hot water. Franz told a story of his father's visit to Louisiana, and re-told, at my request, tales of his father's fondness for cooking exotic foods and seeking out spices from an Italian woman whose shop he loved to visit. "Father pressed his culinary experiments on me, most often when he didn't like his results. Otherwise, he would enjoy the dishes himself!" We had a thoroughly pleasant evening. Franz and Els enjoyed the guests, and Franz invited them to pay him a visit soon at Seestrasse, which pleased them enormously. My friendship with Elton and Ella went back several years, and I was pleased to be able to introduce them to Franz and Els under such pleasant circumstances. I shall always recall the evening with great pleasure.

The next morning, I spent some time with Els, recalling our pleasures of the previous day and making plans for my care of her household for the remainder of the week. She was leaving in the afternoon to visit her sister-in-law. We enjoyed a pleasant breakfast together, and a friend of hers, Lori Hagenback, dropped in to share a book on Picasso. Lori was stately and beautiful, and once again I was warmly greeted by yet another Swiss lady who was neither austere nor distant toward me but openly shared stories of her travels, her family, and her interest in art. More quickly personal than I had come to expect, she also shared painful and sweet recollections of her deceased husband, the anniversary of whose death was a few days away.

After she left, my thoughts remained with her, so I took the time to write her.

Dear Lori,   *April 5th*

I wanted to write to you and extend my greetings to you as you experience, again, the yearly tribute to your dead husband on April 8th. It was such a pleasure to meet you and to feel the depth of your love to your husband, which shines from your beautiful brown eyes as you speak of the sweetness of your life with him. As I told you, this expression I experienced from you rekindled my own consciousness of the strong, sweet love I have been given with my own dear partner and be reminded to love every day we have together, as our later years settle on us softly, with the whisper that there will one day be a parting. You gave me a lovely gift of your own spirit, and I join you in a moment of salute, on April 8th, for the gift of human love, and its meaning in our lives.

Please know you have an admiring and grateful friend, far away, in America.

With fondness, Mary Dian

I walked to the Institute around 10:30 to work in the library, grateful to have some time with the thesis of the Healing Image of the Mare. "The symbol of the feminine principle is the mare; an acceptance of our fate and implies having had the courage to surrender the power attitude of the ego to follow the wisdom of a greater power." And another note: "The mare, Ishtar in Semitic and Babylonian literature, expressing in ourselves a way which is in harmony with our nature, true to self and others." I made as many notes as time allowed before noon when the library closed for lunch. I had hoped to take an article with me for the remaining days, but it was not allowed. The image of the mare, however, remained with me the rest of the week, particularly since I had noticed the great white horse painting at Seestrasse on Tuesday. An image of a white horse is always a comforting reminder for me to trust my own intuition.

After a quick and delicious lunch at the Sonne Hotel, I walked back to Els's house in time to make my farewell before she left. She had prepared a little gift for me with a snapshot of Niko and a pretty bottle of cologne to take home. Els reminded me to take the remaining salmon and salad to Franz's house for supper. She also urged me to move along firmly with my project, and before driving off to visit her sister with little Niko, she left me with feelings of deeper gratitude to her than I could express. I realized once again how my project would have been impossible without her. She left around 2:30 P.M. I fixed a cup of tea and sat to read the letter Els had received for me from her friend Lori Hagenback, in response to the encouraging note I had sent to her.

Dear Mary Dian,

Thank you so much for your lovely card and understanding words. I had rather a difficult day on the 8th. It was raining the whole day and nobody here to cheer me up. But in the end, I have to realize that I must consider myself happy in my comfortable home and with my darling grandchildren to visit me now and then.

It was so nice to meet you at Els's flat. It is really beautiful to join new friends at my age, and I hope to meet you each time you come to Switzerland. In the meantime, I wish you every happiness in your interesting profession.

With my best wishes, yours, Lori Hagenback

I couldn't help but be pleased and gratified by her kindness, especially since she had only just met me.

CHAPTER EIGHT

WE TALK OF FAMILY

❋

I BUSIED MYSELF WITH THE ERRANDS NECESSARY TO MY DEPARTURE, scheduled for the next day; shopped for floral gifts to be delivered to Franz and Els the following week; purchased small, beautifully painted Easter eggs for friends at home; and made a final visit to the Jung Institute for reference materials. Franz was due to pick me up at 3:00 P.M. This time, he drove toward the north and passed by three houses he had built. He parked in front of one large house to tell me the story of his purchase of this choice property for a man and woman from Geneva who had contracted him to design and build a house. But at some juncture, the woman decided not to continue in the belief that Franz would not let her have her own ideas. Realizing that he had perhaps failed to inspire the necessary confidence required, he promised not to say no to any of her wishes.

We then drove past the house of his sister Helene, about which he'd spoken earlier in the week. After the death of her husband, Helene had Franz plan some remodeling for her to accommodate a separate apartment suitable for a rental.

From there, Franz drove east of Tobel to a hillside where he parked, and we set off on foot on the path he had chosen for our walk. Off the path on my right, I was comforted to once again see a white horse, placidly munching hay. The lines from an old Christmas song ran through my head, "The horse knows the way to carry the sleigh through the white and drifted snow . . . " The image of a white horse is a comforting reminder for me to trust my own intuition on how I proceed, no matter how much I fear or worry about this work with Franz. It is a symbol of the feminine principle and acceptance of our fate and having the courage to surrender the power of ego to follow the wisdom of a greater power. A bit further on, we met a lady walking with three beautiful black dogs and a golden retriever, all healthy and energetic, playing as they kept pace with the lady. As we climbed a hillside, the peak of a pyramid structure appeared, and

Franz asked me to guess its purpose. I said I had no idea unless it was a church of some sort. Franz laughed. Soon we were in a garden and the full structural design was visible as a contemporary chapel, and at one side, a new cemetery, immaculately kept with lovely flowers growing at each headstone. "Marianne's husband rests here," Franz said. We wandered around the well-kept plots, admiring the many flowering bushes.

Back in the car, Franz drove to a pretty pond with wild water birds in their natural habitat. As we walked along the pond's path, Franz told me his sister Agathe had a great love of animals. She was the one who had pets of every description. As on previous walks, Franz chose animals, birds, plants, trees, and flowers as his topics of conversation, sharing his knowledge of their ways. I knew the most serious conversation for which I had been preparing myself was still ahead. Earlier, on my way back to Els's apartment after lunch, I considered how Franz must have been trying to come to terms with the idea that I was serious about writing a piece on his life that would one day be published. I knew I would have difficulty coming to terms with the project if he was not able to accept it, and I suspected he realized that as well.

While walking with Franz, I found myself humming, ever so quietly, the words of an old hymn, "Guide thou my feet that I may take thy path, O Lord" and felt a quiet repose enter my consciousness once again, which helped me from time to time as I moved this project forward. Whatever else transpired, I knew this task was guided not solely from ego and would proceed. I hoped, however, for his acceptance.

At one point, in the years ahead, I had a conversation with a psychiatrist in Kansas City who had been a member of the audience during an evening presentation for a discussion group of psychotherapists and others involved in the therapeutic world. I had spoken briefly about my connection with Franz Jung and had mentioned how I admired and enjoyed my friendship and time with Franz and his lady friend, Els Glasser. At the close of our meeting, the psychiatrist said to me, "You know something about Carl Jung that others do not know, and you must write about your experiences with Franz Jung." I was encouraged once again to bring this story to a suitable manuscript.

We returned to the Seestrasse house around 4:30 for a tour of the famous gardens and were greeted by a wonderful dog, a cross between an Irish wolfhound and a Bergermaster sheepdog. Franz introduced me to this bouncy and happy and HUGE creature. This is the animal that belongs to Andreas's family, who also occupy the family house.

We began at the south garden near the ground-level sunroom. Here is the ginkgo tree sent to Carl Jung from his students at the time of Emma's death. At the base of the tree stood the large stone he had carved on. Nearby, the statue of an oriental man, leaning on a hoe, kept guard under a branch of the ginkgo. The inscription, translated from the Latin, reads, "In Modest Harmony with Nature." Franz again spoke of the difficult months following Emma's death when his father was in deep grief. He found no comfort in either his work or painting in the Red Book. It was then that Franz purchased the sizable stone and presented it to his father. Soon, Carl Jung was working with the stone, which helped him with his grieving process. "By springtime, Father was once again able to work and began additional work at Böllingen with more stone carvings and an addition."

Franz then took me to a mysterious stone carving placed over the burial place of his last beloved dog, Jogi. "He was my friend for fifteen years," Franz said. We walked to the little garden house with its brick floor where the early mosaics were made with colored mortar. "Father also used this spot for analysis with his patients when the weather was fine," he said. A sea wall provided a pleasant, sheltered place where the family would often drink coffee. Here Franz and his father constructed the little village. The remains of a castle lie here on the seawall with the composition arches from Franz's childhood building set still encased in the mortar.

The boathouse contained a row boat, a blue dinghy, and a canoe. Franz's sailboat is now used by the postman's son.

As we strolled along the water's edge, Franz pointed out the two great poplars, nicely trimmed. The one nearest the lane, struck by lightning on the night of Jung's death, called to me, and I placed my hand on the cool, craggy bark for a moment. I picked up a brown curl of poplar wood that had tumbled to the ground years before and asked if I could keep it. Franz nodded yes.

I have it still.

The plane tree, the ginkgo, the maple, the poplar that cracked the night Jung died, the elm, the oak, and the Italian cypress all sat in commanding silence. A fine evening mist lay in the air as we returned to the house. We were greeted once more by the huge and happy dog belonging to Andreas's family.

Franz had prepared another *apfelkuchen* and fixed tea, and soon we were comfortably settled in the library. Franz went right to the point. "As I said, your dream that you told me about on Tuesday speaks well for you, but you must tell me your plan and why you are doing this." Some impulse beyond my understanding had led me to tell Franz the dream that had come shortly after my previous summer studying at the Institute. In the dream, I saw a bookstore with a sign in the window that said, "Help Wanted. Inquire Within." I entered the shop and Emma and Carl Jung were there. Both greeted me warmly, but it was Emma who said, "Yes, you must come to work here." But not as a clerk, rather I was to be part of the board. Carl Jung agreed and smiled. Emma, in the dream, sat behind a table or counter where there were many books about Jung, but Carl Jung stood beside me, and we talked eye-to-eye, although, as I recalled the dream later, he would have towered over me as I am a small woman. I had told Franz this dream was important to me and helped me continue my contact with him.

I explained as best I could. "I intend to write about you, Franz, because I believe in the importance of your life, both as your father's son and helper, and as a man who has lived with this heritage on his own terms. I believe a record of Franz Jung is important. It's also true that my own personal history of a young seventeen-year-old woman who left Stuttgart in great grief in 1947 came back around for me in this task. I had become a young journalist, enormously interested in everything I saw and felt in Germany. I had, in a sense, come alive to a part of me during that time. This task brought me back to that part of me that I left behind. All of my studies of Carl Jung are also engaged somewhat, although my perspective—in other words, this project—is taken more as a journalist and less as a Jungian psychotherapist. I feel our friendship has grown quite naturally through common interests and fortuitous chance. I knew from our first meeting I wanted to write about you, but I did not know exactly why or for what purpose, except that it stirred in me my old love for European people and an excitement related to my early awakenings, as a young girl, of what European culture, art, music, and civilian life were all about, hinged to the awakening of peace after the horrors of World War II. Alongside that was a recall of what attitudes and food habits had been for me before that terrible war. I have no agenda except to follow the project as far as possible and write about it honestly. One must go where there is an opening of pleasure and excitement with psyche. That's my story, as best I know. I only understand it is very comfortable and interesting to talk with you, and it seems so for you as well."

Franz nodded. "Yes, it is so. Just so. Now, where would you like to begin?" And with that, Franz launched into a singular monograph, as if the garden walk had readied him to share his thoughts and memories.

•

Marianne's husband, Walter, is still alive. Her death in 1965 was a great sadness for the family. Franz talked of his concern regarding the future of the house after his death: who might carry on, as he has, the task of caring for the library, answering correspondence, entertaining visitors. The first and most logical succession, in terms of knowledge about C. G.'s work would be Lorenz, the youngest, who is an analyst. However, he is unmarried, very ill with cancer, and unable to accept the challenge of taking over. Andreas's wife, Verena, helped the ailing Lorenz finish editing Carl Jung's *Kindertraume*, a large and complicated book. It has just been published in German and will stand as his contribution. Christof, the eldest, is very introverted and content with his practice of architecture, happily settled, and uninterested in this task. Peter, the second son, lives comfortably with his wife, Olga, and is busy with his practice. Andreas, who lives here at Seestrasse, is the likely one. He works with restoration and history for Canton Zurich and is very busy. He keeps the family archives, but his finances would not enable him to purchase the house. As it stands now, the house is under Historic Preservation for the town of Küsnacht and has first refusal for the sale of the house. Canton Zurich owns many public buildings—five churches, two universities, and the Burgholzli Hospital. The town is governed by nine leaders. If they should refuse to purchase the house at its considerable value, then it would go to Franz's heirs. If they should buy it, then of course nothing could be changed, but the question troubles him somewhat. And so, the question of the Seestrasse house is unclear, although the fate of the property is largely secure through the family corporation. The chairman of the family affairs is Lutz Niehaus, Agathe's oldest son. It is he who assists the family in making decisions regarding the care of Böllingen.

I told him I had read somewhere that phenomena such as telekinesis are often connected to the presence of a quiet young woman in early adolescence, and I had wondered if the presence of Carl Jung's sister Gertrud, who died at a young age, had ever been associated with the unexplained incidents of the split table and the shattered bread knife that Carl Jung recorded in *Memories, Dreams, Reflections*. Franz replied no—most often his Grandmother Emilie's presence and her interest in spiritualism was mentioned in regard to those events. I asked Franz for his recollection of these two women. He smiled and launched into stories he had earlier told me: his grandmother lived in a house nearby on Obere Heslibachstrasse maintained by the family. She was a delight for him and his younger sister Helene to visit, and they often stopped by on their way home from school. Grandmother was fascinating to the children because of her grumblings about spirits whom, she said, invaded her kitchen and upset things. The two children played bad jokes on her and she scoffed at their nonsense. There was a glassed-in veranda on the front of the house that Grandmother used as her sleeping room. Franz once more told the story of his grandmother pasting white Star of David, cut from paper, on the door, and each morning checking to see if the seal was broken. On the days when seals were broken, she would grumble about their intrusions and impudence and unwelcome visits while plying the children with fresh baked biscuits or other treats after school. All this was deliciously mysterious for the children. As for Aunt Gertrud, his father's sister, Franz had less affection. She was not "sporty," he said. She couldn't walk far, swim, or enjoy family outings, and was apt to complain a great deal. She lived in a house across the street from Grandmother Emilie with a companion whom Franz called "meager" and the children named "The Spider" because she was very thin and wore a pince-nez. Gertrud died at age fifty or fifty-five, he said.

Somehow, we got on the subject of why he thinks people don't move away from Switzerland easily, and if they do, they are "long remembered." He then told me the story of an ancestor of Lilly's. He was a maker of steel knives and built a fine factory to produce steel blades and swords. For some unknown reason, the story goes, he locked up his fine factory one day in 1814 and left town, moving to France, near Chatel in the French Alps, leaving the key to the factory with a family member. A grandson, visiting the old town many years after his grandfather's death, found, to his surprise, a citizen of the town who, upon hearing the family name, Merker, took the grandson to his grandfather's factory, still locked, and waiting for him to claim it. So he did.

"If Swiss people move away," Franz said, "they are apt to return, one way or another."

The phone in the office rang, and Franz went to answer it. He returned from the call to share good news from a friend, LuAnn, who had called to tell him she had been accepted at the Institute to train as an analyst. This pleased him, and we poured more tea and ate another serving of *apfelkuchen*, in celebration of LuAnn's success.

I asked him if he enjoyed a relationship with members of his mother's family, the Rauschenbachs. Franz immediately began to speak of his favorite aunt, Margaret, from Schaffhausen, Emma's younger sister by two years. "A woman of fine taste," Franz said. She became his confidante as he grew into young manhood. She had three sons, the eldest of whom was Franz's age, and she was apt to chastise her sons with remarks like, "Why can't you be more like Franz?" Franz confessed that at the age of eighteen, he was somewhat of a dandy and felt some resistance to sharing his escapades with his mother and father. But Margaret always provided him with a sympathetic understanding. He then turned to a story about his friend Francis Slocomb, who now lives in Virginia. At some time while Francis was in Küsnacht, she broke her leg, and Franz took Lilly's wheelchair for her to use. Shortly after her studies were finished at the Institute, she lived for a brief period in the Seestrasse house while she made plans to return to the States. I came to believe it is very important for Franz to be helpful where he can and lend assistance with whatever he can do for those he claims as friends, particularly those who are drawn to Küsnacht to study Jung. It's his way, perhaps, of helping the work along, and his gift to his father's memory.

"I was given, by my parents, somewhat of a free life. I grew like a small tree, a little wild and unprincipled. No one asked me what time I came home, or if I had written my compositions for school. I was just accepted, and around, but the household was so busy that I did what I pleased. For example, what sort of a family would have allowed me to own my own motorcycle without anyone even knowing it?

"It was not that I felt I had displeased my parents. In fact, I always felt that I was totally accepted, and I knew that I pleased my father. Perhaps that is why I never felt any great ambition in my own career, but preferred to work on a small scale without taking on partners to build a large architectural firm. At any rate, I recall that as a family, we were probably not too closely integrated with each other.

"Much later, when I found myself to be the father of four sons, I went to my father and said, 'How shall I be a father to these boys?' Carl Jung replied, 'You should let them alone, they will grow up like trees. Be happy none of them is a Dooble, a simpleton.' I realized this was his attitude about his own children as well!

"My sons feel that I am stern. I feel that I have been quite free with them. But of course they needed to accept their responsibilities. Lilly and I had our difficulties with them. Andreas was a teaser, and once I secured him with a seat belt to insist that he finish his soup. He remembers that. Perhaps, I was not always adequate. Andreas had difficulties with his glands, and Lorenz also. They both had to be taken out of school for a time. We finally sent them to finish school at Davos before entering Techniche Hochschule—Andreas at my school in Stuttgart, and Lorenz and Peter in medicine here in Zurich."

•

We broke for a pleasant supper of Bircher muesli, with cheese, bread, the rest of Els's salmon, and the remaining bananas foster sauce, spooned over ice cream. As Franz lay out our dinner, we discussed the making of the great cheeses in Switzerland. Franz told me of farmers taking the cows to the mountains and the making of cheeses in huge copper pans kept through the winter in mountain shelters.

I recalled for Franz a procession of this annual pilgrimage in the early spring of my first visit. My husband and I had traveled up to St. Galen and watched as all the cows, scrubbed clean, their horns festooned with flowers, and the great bells clanging round their necks walked up the path. "Yes," said Franz. "That is a good place to make such cheese." With that, we cut another bite of the emmentaler we were enjoying. During our supper, we had a lovely discussion of Stuttgart, my beloved, although brief, home after WWII.

As we began to clean up after our supper, Franz mentioned bicycle trips with his father. I asked him to recall them for me. The trips, lasting two to three weeks, occurred in three successive years—1921, '22, and '23 when Franz was 13, 14, and 15 years respectively. The first visit was along the Po River toward Venice, the second east to Palmas, and the third to the Lake of Galdar.

> We enjoyed seeing the ruins together in Padua and Verona. There is a town on an island with a castle in the middle near Turin, like a mandala. We traveled the moraines and very straight roads built in the time of Napoleon, seven times up and down, and made the enormous climb of 300 meters for a splendid view. Father was very interested in all the geologic formations, rivers, erosions, and boulders. At Turin, we visited the famous pilgrimage church of the seventeenth century.
>
> Father also showed me the red light district. I was then fourteen years old and asked the meaning of the red lanterns. He warned me, "Don't go there."

I wondered if he had reached back into his old journals to recall these factual and accurate notes, or if these memories were so embedded in him that he was able to tell the stories accurately. It was past 10 P.M. when Franz drove me back to my room at Els's. We were both quite tired. There would be one more day with Franz, and I wondered what would be in store for me.

CHAPTER NINE

Our Final Day

✵

I WOKE EARLY AS THERE WERE SEVERAL THINGS I NEEDED TO complete before leaving for the airport, including packing. Rather than go out, I fixed a cup of Kaffee Hag with milk and sat to write a letter for Els to find when she returned home.

Dear Els,

What a splendid gift you have given to me this week from your warm and hospitable heart as you offered me every conceivable access to your lovely home, your time, and your interest in the project I have undertaken with Franz. Even as you labored to be sensitive to me, using the English language for me, which, while you managed beautifully, I understood that the greatest subtleties of your fine intellect and the nuances of your highly discriminating sensitivity were difficult to convey. I am embarrassed that I have not made better progress with my German and have vowed to attempt this task once again when I return to my home, in the hope that there might be another meeting for us, and I can speak to you in a German that is still going to be rudimentary, even at my best.

As time goes on and the "soup" we are stirring with Franz develops, I must try to explain to you that this project to write about Franz can only grow to whatever fulfillment the vicissitudes of time, chance, and circumstance allow. It must evolve with a sense of unfolding, like the white tulips, in its own way. I have committed myself, only as providence allows, with the understanding, also, that I have a first commitment to my husband and family, a second to my practice, a third to my studies, and perhaps a fourth to my music. For me, these must be kept in their proper order. I believe Franz

Jung deserves a place in the literature of the Jungian community. I admire his place as a quiet Swiss opinion in the world, and somehow there seems to be a trust between us that is the container of an honest exchange and flow in freedom. I also believe that without you, what might have been a passing notice of him can take hold and be a healthy threshold from which any biography must work. So here we are, the three of us, in this "soup." There must be a fourth element to balance the equation. In Jungian terms, I believe that fourth dimension is some sort of faith, that which is to be done will be done in its own way and cannot be manipulated other than by the careful use of the resources each of us brings to the task. JAMBALAYA is a good metaphor... the American native brings to the Swiss kitchen some adaptation, some spices, and requires some good cooperation, hospitality, and the intuition, yes, of its own accord, to cook what we have together and let it simmer once the ingredients are in place. I do not feel that I chose this project. In effect, it has chosen me. Franz, and even your dear little dog-spirit of Niko, who wants only to be connected, have been given the task to try and bring this forward. Perhaps those factors are the most powerful. Two male, two female, a good grouping perhaps. We can only wait, and see, and remain awake, as best we can, responsive to each other. Thank you for your loving gift of a generous heart and spirit to so many people.

I do not know when, or ever if, I can return. Only the work knows. But I do hope to see you once again. I told Franz and my friends that I would like to take you home with me. What that means is that I need to take your spirit, love, and attention to Franz and his life back to Kansas City. So this project remains infused with your own creativity, spontaneity, and energy, combined with mine.

Please take good care of your dear self! We all four know the ghosts of time. And we all four try to live as long as we can—you, me, Franz, and Niko.

Fondly, Mary Dian

After folding the letter and propping it where Els would be sure to see it, I sat for a moment and thought about what a lovely friend she had become. I recalled how she loved flowers and kept them in her apartment. One morning, we had walked in her small garden and exchanged German, Swiss, and English names for the beauties as we came upon them, singing them back and forth, repeating their names in each other's language. And I thought at the time what a fine Swiss-German lesson this was. I was especially fond of the word for peonies—*pfingst rosen*. I don't expect to ever forget that word. It was also the morning when she took me to the fence and introduced me to Christof's dogs, which wagged themselves all over to greet us. The next morning, Els's friend Laurie came to visit and share her book on twentieth-century art. She, too, seemed very relaxed with me and not at all shy about my being an American, for which I was duly pleased. She later wrote me a kind letter, which I still have. After she left, Els prepared another lunch for us of smoked salmon, Swiss brown bread, cheese, onions, and capers, a choice Swiss lunch.

During lunch, Els spoke at length of her own life, her deceased husband, their home, and her own sadness at not being able to have children. She showed me early photographs, one especially I remember— she and her husband in evening dress, looking very smart indeed.

I also shared my husband and my experience, and how simpler it was for me and my own marriage because of my husband's entering the analytical process also and working along with me on dream material. I also remember thinking that Els herself had a sensitive understanding of Carl Jung's work and his contribution to the world. I was also aware of how Els had encouraged Franz to offer his hospitality, for so many years, to those who still come to his family door after his father's death. She was a strong supporter for Franz in that important task over the years. I sighed. I would miss her. But now it really was time for me to finish packing before Franz arrived to take me to the airport.

We were quiet during the drive of some fifteen miles, exchanging a few pleasantries, pointing out a fine building or farm as we passed them. Franz would not agree to drop me off and insisted on parking and helping me inside with my luggage and walking me down the aisle to the gate. He could go no farther and so stopped as I went through the turnstile and started down the ramp. On impulse, I stopped and turned. To my surprise and pleasure, Franz still stood where I had left him. We both raised a hand at the same moment in farewell. I then turned and walked onto the plane.

PART TWO

It is time to begin this second part, all of which is based on correspondence conducted by mail. I am re-entering this project late in my life because it doesn't leave me to rest in peace without bringing this story of Franz Jung and Els Glasser to its ultimate conclusion.

CHAPTER TEN

LETTERS

❋

Dear Mary Dian,   April 24, 1990

Time has rushed on since you left here on the 7th of April. I had all days "something on my hands or up my sleeve." Visitors again coming and going. Nice visit on Easter at Olga and Peter's, and on E. Monday also Andreas together with Olga's father who has the same age as myself. He is a simple but clever man with a lot of humor, and as he had only a wife and three daughters and one son, he once upon a time just walked away from his home duties. He is owner of two apartments high in Mt. Valais out for grazing costs as he lives in Bern. But in summertime it is very romantic to live in such a hut at about 6,000 feet height, a bit uncomfortable and somewhat cold, but the cow bells all day and night about gives you company and for some Swiss the feeling of being close to nature! We have still no real spring, cold, rainy and heavy clouds, but today I saw the first time in my reeds before the house on the shore a duck with three ducklings not older than 2–3 days. They breed somewhere near the water, in the boathouse or under the bushes near the lake and then one day, I wonder! They are all in the water, lively and the mother extremely wonderful and caring. The male duck is not so important. Sometimes he keeps away other ducks or water birds in the first days, later he is no more interested in his family. But the female keeps her brood together till they are well grown up. Now I had a letter from my friend Francis Slocomb from Virginia Beach. She has again plans to leave there for a better place. She wrote me that she would prefer to work at a university as she did some years ago, to teach on Jungian Psychology, and beside that write for journals in that branch and eventually having also some patients. Her situation in Virginia Beach is not too well based, as she can not find enough clients to live by such an income. She is a widow with not much money in the background. She should find a place where she would have a regular income which would give her the chance to write and teach, which I am sure she could do very good. Thought I could give your address to Francis in the case she would consider also to come to Kansas City. I do not know if this could be a temptation or not, but I just wanted to know if you could be interested in such a possibility. Next Saturday comes my friend Karen Helhoase from Denver. She is touring Italy to get some real impressions for her new book about painting. In May is announced Dr. Tom Kirtch from San Francisco, Murry Stein, and Dr. Thidd from Chicago for a visit at Böllingen, which I cannot deny. At the end of May, Els and myself are again at the Isle of Sardinia. As she most probably has not yet written a letter for you, she sends you her warm most greetings. Your gift flower is still in bloom. Many thanks for that fine gift.

With kindest regard, Franz

Dear Mary Dian,   May 11, 1990

Many thanks for your letter. I feel happy that you came safely back to your family and to your work, and that also for you, life is going on as it should. I send you some pictures of your visit in early April. Els is very proud of her photographer's skill, and I think these pictures are a very nice remembrance of our discussions. You look very photogenic is that red jacket! Els sends you her best greetings.

Now to your project to present me to the literature. I have no enthusiasm at all; on the contrary, I hate it. I just refuse to join in for such a work, sorry. It is not shyness as you think. I know what I am and what not. And if I want to become mentioned in literature or anywhere in public, it is my business, certainly not yours. You have much more vital and important work to write about that are of interest and necessary for public life and the world. Earth will keep on turning around also without Franz Jung being mentioned—that everybody is sure about. So my dear, Mary Dian, please do not set aside your work because of thinking about me, and what questions you would asking me in due future, and look for other trips instead east to Europe in the fall, better to west, there are also lying secrets in China or Australia which are far more worth to be found and described, and take your husband with you, he will enjoy seeing a part of the world that he probably has not yet visited.

The last weeks were rather busy, I had a nice visit by Karin, the woman from Denver. She passed on her way to Italy, 2 days at Küsnacht. She was lucky as we had two perfect, sunny and warm spring days, so we had two beautiful walks along a little lake on the other hillside and through the beautiful beech-woods with the young leaves. Four days later I had visitors, one a teacher of a Koran school in Spain, at tea, and not unexpected by myself, a discussion of Jung's ideas was nearly impossible, because neither they knew much of Jung, nor myself had any knowledge of Mohammed's philosophic ideas. Today I had Dr. Tom Kirsch with his wife from California and Dr. Mudd from Chicago for an afternoon at Böllingen. Unhappily, it was a cold and rainy day, so the place was rather gray and cool, which suited the introverted architecture not at all bad. I guess they were all the same much impressed about the meaning of such a work, in which my father had invested so much energy and spirit and unconsciousness. What a difference of our time, compared with 4000 years earlier ideas in Egypt where they constructed for their dead, things and gods of realizations in stone. We are extreme barbarians in mind and in practice. I just read through some reports of 1930 excavations in Egypt. Excuse my going away from our subject.

Let me close, I want to post this letter early that you do no take decisions which will complicate the situation even more.

Kindest regards, Franz

Needless to say, this was a disturbingly forthright letter. I imagine I wrote a suitable response. However, in retrospect, I found his letter upsetting at the time and am pleased to have found a copy of a longer response marked "not sent." Perhaps I only sent the first two paragraphs to him.

Dear Franz   July 24, 1990

I apologize for my delay in responding to your letters of April 24th and May 11th. It has taken me some time to assimilate the content of the last one, and also to make inquiries related to the first one.

Regarding your question concerning your friend Francis Slocomb, in the event that she might wish to make a change, I would be happy to discuss the opportunities here with her. I mentioned this matter to Gary Hartman, our resident analyst, who recalled visiting with Ms. Slocum shortly after her return to the States, at which time she was considering both the East and the West Coasts. Another member of our group met her this summer at a conference in New Mexico and mentioned what a pleasant and attractive person she seemed to be. If she decided to locate permanently in Kansas City, we would see that she is warmly received, and try to provide her with client referrals. However, securing a teaching post would require considerable time and effort on her part, since there are not always academic posts readily available. My husband and I taught an introductory course in Jungian Psychology at a local seminary last spring which we enjoyed very much, but the work was done more out of love than for financial return since the stipend was meager at best. The permanent posts in the field of Psychology are fairly complete at this time as far as I know.

Your letters reflect a busy spring with many interesting guests. I know this is a pleasure for you, but it is also gracious of you to provide so many people with the wonderful opportunity of visiting your home and the Böllingen Retreat. Here things are, as usual, very busy. In addition to my practice, there are plans for me to develop a psychodrama for in-patients at two local psychiatric hospitals, hopefully in the fall, a nice addition for me to combine my theatre skills with psychotherapy.

Also, our family will assemble in August at the beach near Charleston, S.C. to celebrate Warren's and my 40th anniversary. I'm sure you understand how the ocean has "Barrier Islands." Our island is called Isle of Palms. Warren's brother and his wife will join us. There will be nearly 30 family members and friends, so we are looking forward to it very much, and planning parties and games. We also plan to enjoy the great Spoleto Festival which was established some years ago by Gian Carlo Menotti. Many illustrious musicians will perform during the week, so it should be a splendid, if short, vacation for us. I sang several years in two Menotti operas, and I have a fondness for his work.

We experienced fierce spring floods this year here in Missouri. While our house has remained free of invading waters, many friends and clients have suffered, so we have made the house and our functioning laundry available for those whose homes have been inundated. There has been too much water, and an outbreak of illnesses in the city which is apt to accompany flood waters. Nature, in Missouri, is an untamed constant challenge. Either there is too much or not enough.

My work goes well. I have several new clients and invitations from two local psychiatric hospitals to establish programs in psychodrama, about which we talked during my last visit. I dearly love doing this work, and hope only that I can respond to the requests and still conduct my own practice with enough time to ponder the needs of my people. Warren works in a different manner, with a longer history of experience working with people's marital problems. He is able to accommodate 40 hours a week of therapy, while I am reeling at 25 to 30. But then, I work in a different manner than he does.

I had another interesting experience this spring. I designed and directed a play-reading presentation of the "Simpleton's Scenes" from Shakespeare's "A Midsummer Night's Dream." These scenes were performed on Midsummer Night in a beautiful rustic garden here in the city. The scenes, you may recall, are the little comic plays within the play, and made a lovely evening of theatre. I have been working each Midsummer Night (June 15th) on this project for perhaps ten years, editing the scenes and arranging the material so it flows smoothly. Also, of course, I must address your wishes, expressed in your letter of May 11th. It was very clear that you are not comfortable regarding my project on you and your father, and so I must respect your wishes and not trouble you with plans to develop a manuscript further at this time. Experience tells me that it is not wise to work forcefully with life, but better to let things flow naturally, in "modest harmony with nature," as you so aptly say. We must, then, agree to let this manuscript rest. But I would be sad, indeed, to lose contact with you and Els, or discredit our friendship, which has been so rich for me.

Thank you so much for the fine photographs! Els does a very nice job with her camera, indeed, as you commented. You look quite fit and healthy sitting there together. My fond best wishes to you, Franz, and of course to dear Els as well. Please thank her for the excellent photographs.

Warm Regards, Mary Dian

Dear Mary Dian,   *August 5, 1990*

Thank you very much indeed for your letter of July 24th and the tapes with the wonderful music of the Mormon Tabernacle Choir. Your tapes have arrived for me at the right moment: I am listening to Bach and Handel . . . and I am crying and have a very heavy heart: Franz's son Lorenz, in since a month at the hospital in Männedorf, died last night! – For Franz it is awful and he needs all my help in this time of mourning. We are both very very sad. Dear Mary Dian, please understand that I cannot write you more at the moment. And you certainly understand now why Franz was not able to accept your proposition to finish your project. I still remember the pleasant time of your visit in Küsnacht, I like the picture of you and your husband, and I like your cat, and I still have your flower pot.

With all my love, Els (and Niko)

Dear Mary Dian,   *August 8, 1990*

Thank you for your nice note and the picture of the satiated squirrel. Glad to hear that all is going so well your way. Things in Kansas City sound like they are really popping these days. I hope that it is not as hot there as here. We are having a regular heat wave this past couple of weeks here. Temperatures are at or over 100 degrees daily. That is really something for us as we have never seen/experienced such a hot time here before.

We have not been over to see Franz Jung. We ran into Els Glaser a couple of times out walking her dog. Franz was quite busy for a while and then took off for an extensive vacation to Sardinia. We did not hear from him when he got back, so I wrote to him. I just heard from him in the last week or so, and it is not a good time to come around to visit with him. Perhaps sometime this fall we will see if we can get together.

We are doing well. I am writing to you on paper from the post office, where Ella is spending some time these days although there is no sleet or snow to impede her getting the mail out and there has been very little rain. She is doing fine, enjoying the work and the early morning cool to be out walking in. She sends her greetings to you.

Happy Anniversary. Sounds like a gala time in spite of the crowd. That part of South Carolina is nice. We made it there once on our way to Charleston to go to some of the Spoleto Festival there. I don't know what the coast looks like there now after their devastating hurricane. I wish you the best. It is wonderful to have a 40th anniversary. Congratulations to you and Warren and have a wonderful time.

We still plod along here. I am beginning work on my thesis and keep my fingers crossed that the writing will go well. I have not done anything like that in a while and right now remember what it felt like to labor over a dissertation. While this is not one of those, it is in the ballpark and I hope that it goes okay over the next months.

Thank you again for your note. Have a good end of the summer.

With warmest regards, Elton Squires

Dear Mary Dian,   September 9, 1990

Thank you very much for your letter, Aug. 24th which is full of warm feelings.

It is really an awful thing to lose a son, well, he was a man in his best age of 47 and it is not just the point to speak of "a son." He was very, even too detached, since many years, even so during lifetime of my wife. I think it began when he was going away from home about age 16 or 18, but later returned for three years again, during his time at the Technical School. But later he preferred to have his own little flat for the most part of his student-time and later as a micro-biologist went in some way concealed from Mother and Father and his next relatives.

So it came that my wife and myself missed the best part of that son's life, and only in the last years of his mother's illness he came regularly, weekly, to talk with his mother. I was more or less excluded from those conversations, and thinking of the extreme discretion my wife offered, I had very little insight in the development of that young man. It changed only after death of my wife in 1983, when Lorenz and myself became quite good comrades, but our inner circles never crossed each other, occasionally, there was an occasional touch or one felt the near neighborhood!

I only now begin to find together some threads in the very, very complicated net of weaving of his life, going through his files of letters, trying to find out behind a name of a person, who wrote me a very personal letter for condolence, also the personality and the feelings of the writer, who seemed, and was also in reality, the best friend of my son, a human being I had never heard of before.

That makes it a bit difficult for me to realize that for years and years, I stood aside, on "the other side of the trolley," and Lorenz too was in a way on the "other side of a mountain." We only knew for some weeks, or even more, that he is probably still alive, continually on a journey through Spain—England, Yugoslavia, or so but certainly no address.

Thank you very much for the beautifully formulated letter, one sees that you are a gifted writer. Then I was very touched by your good idea to send me that cello-suite by Bach on a tape. It is beautiful and quieting to listen to the deep tones of Yoyo Ma's play. It is a music which fits exactly in my somber mood. To give me a lift, I have at my recorder some impressive tunes. If I can get it on a tape, mine is a C-D disk, I will send it.

On Wednesday I have the Squires couple for tea.

With many thanks, love, Franz

Dear Mary Dian,   October 10, 1990

Some days ago I posted for you a music-tape I mentioned in my letter weeks ago. I hope it will safely reach you. An American singer, Barbara Hendricks, whom I heard several months ago at Zurich, is singing different compositions by Mozart, all 'sacred arias' with that delicate reserve and careful restriction for my taste this special music needs. It gave me a lot of comfort during the long last months of Lorenz's illness and still means much to me, and brings peace and consolation whenever I feel bad. During the last days, I began to sort out my son's letters and manuscripts, giving back some items to friends, dream-materials to clients etc., and I see every day more behind a screen, sides of a man, which I have never known before. He certainly had the qualities to become a very good psychologist, it is really a sad loss to everybody, who had known and worked with him. Yes, his skin was not thick enough and his sensitivity too fine for such a difficult profession. And then he had a lot of resistance, to be reminded that he was a grandson of C. G. J. Never the less he was a very loyal representative of my father's ideas, and was the only one in my family who readily knew and understood the writings of C. G. His resistance was mainly against people, who came to him more or less out of curiosity, to get an impression how a grandson of a famous man is doing his job, not of inner need or deep problems. Lorenz thought always, that a lot of such clients were taking his short time and energy, he had so many projects in his mind, but he had to leave them behind with his dwindling forces.

You certainly know these melodies, but nevertheless, I felt compelled to send some thing meaningful for me to express my gratitude, I was so touched to get your message. My son Andreas has gone to Greece for 14 days of holidays with his whole family a wonderful program, driving through Greece, with the boat through the Aegean to Rhodes and Crete and bathing somewhere in the still sunny and warm clear water of a shore near Cape Sounion, on the foot of a marvelous Poseidon temple-ruins. Els joins me daily, we have a good household together with a rich harvest of fresh vegetables and fruit. With kindest regards and much love from Els. She is busy preparing our lunch.

Franz

Dear Franz,   December 11, 1990

For several weeks I have been trying to set aside a time away from my work and household so that I could spend some quiet hours reading through your last letters and playing the beautiful Mozart Arias without interruption. Finally such a time has arrived. Today. I apologize for such a delay, particularly lest you feel my long silence might reflect a loss by the mail service of the wonderful tape. Not so—it has been a companion in my new car, it has traveled to the seashores of South Carolina with me and my family; it has been shared with my husband's brother, and it is now playing as I write, and I must put down my pen from time to time and simply listen.

I find, Franz, that my experiences with music are certainly not unique, but perhaps a little more understandable for me if I consider inferior function, which is sensation. For example, I prefer to "live" in a certain work for extended periods of time, to hear it, sing it, play it on the cello…perhaps stop what I'm doing in the middle of a task in my kitchen and run to the cello or the piano just to play a little part that is insisting itself to consciousness within my head … and I want no other music until this work has had its time with me.

Singing in a choir is a great help to me this way because although we rehearse excellent music suitable for each week, the choir also studies two or three major works a year and performs them in concert. So I have the opportunity for a total immersion in this manner. Perhaps for people who are by nature sensate, music can be more readily absorbed. But for me it is a long, intense, and very powerful process. So I am careful to be in the music and keep the intellect out of it as much as possible.

AH! That is why it is hard to write about it, and why it has taken me so long to respond and thank you for this beautiful gift and the hours of great pleasure. And because we have begun to understand how this is, I am sending the music of my inner life. It comes to you in two forms—one is for your CD player, a professional recording, and the other with the blue label you will see is for Els's machine and is a nice recording of my performance as a member of St. Andrew's choir. The first piece on the tape is a performance of my good friend, our Choirmaster, David Vogeding, playing a short, lovely organ concerto, then comes the Magnificent Schubert Mass #6 in E flat Minor. It gives me great pleasure to send it to you, and I hope you and Els enjoy it.

This mass is seldom performed by amateur choral groups, in America at any rate, because it is very difficult to sing, but a wonder to do once the music is mastered. Then one is almost inside the soul of Schubert for a time, a splendid garden, indeed.

Elton and Ella Squires were here to stay with us this past week and spoke with great pleasure of their visit with you and of meeting Andreas and his wife. It was enormously kind of you to entertain them, Franz, and I am deeply grateful. They have not fully decided whether to settle here, but they made several calls on people and Ella interviewed for a teaching position. We shall see. They had only a week here, and Swiss Air kept their luggage in Zurich for half of that week in a decompression chamber! So they were without their clothing. There seems to be a collective mood of paranoia in Switzerland these days. I trust that the officials of the airlines will find more likely terrorists than the Squires sooner or later. Thank you also for sharing your thoughts in both letters about the life of Lorenz. I was particularly moved by your analogy of standing on "the other side of the valley" from him. I have hope that his work on the Jung Seminars will soon be translated so that more of the world can benefit from this labor. The stewardship of his Grandfather's work which he demonstrated is very impressive and must be very gratifying for you.

Warren joins me in sending holiday greetings. May the celebration of the season warm your spirits.

Much love to you and to dear Els, Mary Dian

Greetings to you, Els and Franz,   February 3, 1991

Here in Kansas City this day, the crocus bravely push upward from winter sleep toward the still-chill sun, and the north wind whips wildly around the side of my house. I hope this finds you both well and hearty.

It may be that spring stirs in me already, but whatever the reason, I find that I must speak to you both again regarding the hope that remains with me, that I may continue to work on your, Franz's, biographical material. I let the project go for a time in deference to your wishes, and while I know and respect so much your desire to remain a private person, my feeling is that it is not really quite possible. Someone will write a biographical piece about Franz Jung, and my feeling is that perhaps it is still a good idea that it be done while you are able to see to its accuracy. I think it should be written as objectively, factually, and honestly as possible, without intrusive speculation or subjective rumination. And these are my reasons for coming to you once again with this question. While this project is not my life's work by any means, I feel that some peripheral journalistic ability of mine can be well invested here in behalf of the archives. I am also well aware of your feelings of being intruded upon, perhaps. And I do have some sympathy for this. Yet I know Dr. Carl Jung's legacy has only just begun, and his work is rumored to be a powerful conceptual bridge to the 21st Century. Much more will be written, and there are few left to edit from first-hand experience.

A careful look at my own nature shows me that it is not comfortable for me to continue this project without your permission. I talked to my husband, Warren, about it this week, and also my own analyst, and decided to put the question to you once again, knowing that changes do occur in time. Should you say yea or nay, all will be well. I must also keep in mind that someone else may have approached you to write about you whom you favor, and that you two dear people will have many reasons and thoughts about this matter that I can't possibly imagine.

If you do decide that it is appropriate for the project to continue, then I would like to block out some time, perhaps in the fall, to pay a visit so that the parameters of the project can be defined and some clarification accomplished. However this shakes out, you both have my warmest affection and gratitude for many hours of pleasure spent in your splendid company.

Fondly, Mary Dian

Dear Franz,   March 4, 1991

I write bringing you greetings once again from Kansas City, along with hope that this letter finds you in good health and spirits and able to enjoy your daily walks and spring travels with the wonderful lady, Els Glasser. Please give her my warm regards. I recall that it is nearly a full year since I was with you both. That seems impossible. But what a sad and difficult year. Here in the United States there is an air now of flag-waving and rowdy nationalism as the people celebrate the cease fire in the Middle East. Yesterday, which was Sunday, churches all over the country held throngs of people offering thanks to God that most of our troops had been "spared." Much was made of it in the news media. But little is said about the vast numbers of wasted lives left lying in the desert from among the ranks of the poor Iraqis. So things go when chauvinistic and superficial emotionalism have not been subjected to a deeper and more honest human reflection. This whole experience has been very sad and discouraging for many thoughtful Americans. Nevertheless we too are grateful that the hostilities are no longer perpetrating genocide, for whatever comfort that is when one is faced with the reality of such a brutal, selfish, wasteful story added to the record of 20th Century history.

I took a little walk around my still-winter garden this morning and found the first shoots of the lovely and gloriously yellow Osterglocken under the oak leaves. So the mood lifts a little.

Franz, I am sending under separate cover a folio of the work of a dear friend of our family, portrait artist Frank Szasz. He has agreed to accept a modest commission from a few "Friends of Jung" members here in Kansas City to paint a portrait of your father to add to his "Pathfinder" series of world-renown humanitarians. These portraits in the series have been duplicated in print form and sold internationally with good success and have benefited a number of charitable causes. I am pleased that he wishes to add C. G. Jung to the series. He lives already with a comfortable income, so that after his expenses are covered and printing costs underwritten, whatever profits become available will benefit the Jung organizations here.

While I do not want to trouble you needlessly about this project, I did promise my friend, Mr. Szasz, that I would inform you about it. He asked me if I thought there might still be unpublished photographs among the archives, and I replied that I seriously doubted that such would be the case since so many illustrated collections have been published. I did recall, however, that I met a photographer in Zurich in a studio on, I believe, the Limmat Str. who claimed to have been an official photographer of your father during his later years, and this man showed me some unpublished studies at that time.

I cannot recall this photographer's name, and since I would like to put Mr. Szasz in touch with him, I am once again asking you for a little assistance in locating the name. I do hope you know of him, so that Mr. Szasz can contact him prior to his intended trip to Europe which he plans during the month of April.

Once again, I feel I must assure you that I would not trouble you over a project of this nature if I did not have every confidence that the work to be produced would reflect the highest professional quality and be a distinguished product. I believe the folio will convince you of Frank's uncanny ability to produce remarkable likenesses of great people who are no longer living.

Since Frank's schedule is soon underway, I think it would be best if I tried to reach you by telephone fairly soon so that he can make adequate arrangements for his travel plans to include a visit to Zurich, providing we can find the right person to assist him. I shall try to call between 3:00 P.M. and 4: P.M. after March 11th, in hope of reaching you. I do hope this is not too troublesome for you . . . and I also must confess that I am pleased to have a good reason to visit with you briefly once again by telephone.

I look forward to talking with you soon, Fondly, Mary Dian

Dear Franz,   *July 17, 1991*

I hope this note finds you well. It seems a long time since we talked.

I am writing to bring a word that a close family friend, Lawrence Hester, who plans to be in Zurich soon, may call you for a visit or chat. I would be so glad for you to spend a little time with him by telephone. Mr. Hester is the man who joined with Warren and me to commission Frank Szasz to paint the portrait of your father, with the help of you and Els.

Also, he is the owner of Mr. Szasz's original painting of your father.

The little cards bearing the portrait of C. G. have been sold at cost, and all the profits going to societies directly involved in promoting your father's work. While we have had neither time nor efficient office staff to market them very widely, they have generated steady funds that feed back into various "Jungian" organizations world-wide, and the project seems to move on its own momentum.

I encouraged Mr. Hester to call you and bring you my own warm personal greetings. He, I, and many friends of Frank Szasz mourn his tragic death this past March.

While it is not my wish in any way to impose on your resources of time and energy, I would consider it a great personal favor to me if you could visit with him by phone, if possible, even briefly, if you happen to be at home when he calls.

My life is very full with clients, family, and the manuscript to which I am committed, and work with our local Jung society. I still hope, in the future, to make another trip to Europe, but things have not been favorable thus far to make such a plan. We feel very fortunate, in these busy times, to be able to fly every two months or so to our little condo on the Atlantic coast for a brief break and rest by the ocean. Ownership of this vacation apartment is shared with four other partner-owners, all of whom are friends or family members. It sits right beside the ocean.

Sitting on the deck or walking by the mighty sea has been a wonderful break, regularly, for us over the years. The arrangements are made by the group, so that each of us has a share of rotating calendar dates, and the facility holds 6 to 8 people comfortable, not unlike your system at Böllingen with your family.

Fortunately, my health is strong. Warren has suffered the misery of a detached retina in his right eye which required surgery in March and some additional repair work. This has been slow to heal. He had a wretched winter and missed the springtime loveliness entirely, but now seems much better and he is once again his comfortable and amiable dear self.

All is well. Take care.

Fondly, Mary Dian

P.S. Knowing that my friend Larry will soon be in your home encourages me to send along this music, the Schubert Quintet, the musician Yoyo Ma. The second movement is for me above any other music because it brings to me the truth of the Self or Soul, which is the goal of us all. One cannot listen to it, truly, without being stopped and brought to the exquisite reality of the beauty and pathos of human existence. As I listen to it, I am instantly connected to the great Oak tree by my window, and its indomitable spirit of life, in this moment of NOW. Once I had a dream that I could see inside this big tree, and saw an old lady with long gray hair, happily playing her cello. I often think of her. I am certain she is still in there and still playing.

Please enjoy it all, but save the second movement as my special message to you, my noble friend. It is impossible for me to express how much my brief association with you and Els have enriched my life.

Dear Mary Dian,   August 22, 1991

With great pleasure I got your message of July 17th announcing the visit of Lawrence Hester, in fact both came the same day. "Larry," as you call him, called me up early at about 9:00 A.M. As usual, I had difficulties to understand his name, and at eleven your letter came, so I had the necessary introduction for the afternoon of the visit, the same afternoon at three P.M.

I am so sorry for you that Frank Szasz had to die to quickly and unforeseen. You have my deepest sympathy for what that cost. He was a kind man full of life and jokes and deep thought.

After Larry came on Monday I saw him a second time, but only on a very short lunch at Hotel Sonne, together with the group with whom he was traveling. Larry was leading the 15/16 people through Switzerland with a bus visiting all places of importance.

As I could not manage by myself such a crowd, I asked Casey only to come by at three o'clock which he probably did not like so much as he was rather short with me. He was a quarter of an hour in the library and as I did not know either him or his famous grandfather, I had no questions to ask him.

Some of the audience during the lunch were asking those unanswerable and silly questions, as "What did you like best about your father" or "How did your father impress you?" One woman of the group wanted to know about my mother. What can one answer between bites of salad? She certainly was the best mother of all and an exactly fitting wife for such a husband. She had the reins in hand, invisible but effectively, and could lead or stop whenever she would feel neglected or let out of the play of life.

I hope the eyes of your husband could be cured for good. It is really a hard time when he can no more read and see everything daily life demands, and for a man it is so difficult to need help for everything daily life demands.

Happily, I am fairly well off, my eyes are not too bad, at least one is good enough. I can drive without spectacles and the other eye does only help a bit as everything is blurred and cannot be corrected. This long and persistent inflammation of the eyelid is a bit irritating but it is chronic, and I can live with it. To my great surprise, Larry brought the little present from you, the CD: Schubert OP Dp 56 with Yoyo Ma at the cello. Thank you very much for this remembrance of memorable music; it was a nice idea of you to send it to me.

My life is going very very quiet, for, yes, once again some visitors from abroad, letters to places all over the world, and some nice friends whom I see occasionally.

At the end of August there is a congress of International Analytic Psychology people at Zurich, 700-1,000 gathering for a week, and as it happens some of them want to contact me, which it is not exactly my preferred wish. But at least at the opening of the festival at the 20th of August, I must take part. Though the congress is not in honor of CGJ but as it is in Zurich, the management can not avoid to remember CGJ and to invite some of his living descendants. We have a fine summer and beautiful lake here to swim! Give my compliments to your husband and best wishes for you.

Kindest regards, Franz

Dear Franz,   September 9, 1991

I was so pleased to receive your kind letter and delighted that you were able to spend some time with my friend Larry. He has returned from his visit to Switzerland and has taken me to lunch this past Tuesday so that we could share some news of you. He also had some pictures taken at Hotel Sonne, and I was able to have a good look at your image.

Franz, I have not seen you in perhaps four or five years, but you seem not to have aged much at all! Your expression revealed that the occasion was somewhat less than celebrative for you, but I know you have done a worthy service by meeting Larry and visiting with the American tourist group, and introduce them to one of your father's family members.

I believe your father's impact on the history of our culture continues to expand and will reach into our next century as a conceptual bridge to new ways of understanding human behavior. And I must say, also, that every one of us who has sat in that library and visited with you is wiser and better-grounded in the meaning of Carl Jung's work than those who have not. So you have not only done a great service, but conducted it with humility, wit, and grace. And that all came about when you were able to move back into the Seestrasse house after the death of your parents. Of course, I am not telling you anything you have not considered, and I also know something of your natural modesty. But I must tell you, none the less. You have done a very important piece of work in this manner, and please do not equivocate!

I am so pleased that you received the quintet. As I mentioned in the enclosed note, the second movement often accompanies my morning meditations, and I like to hear it when I am entirely alone. I hope that you also find it a powerful and contemplative work. Enclosed is a brochure which I and others have just completed for our Kansas City "FRIENDS OF JUNG" group for the remainder of this year. Our local study groups from 1996 are also listed. Our group is growing rapidly.

Now, my Seminar begins on December 4th (my 66th birthday!) In January, I begin teaching another course at our local Theological seminary, "Carl Jung's Concept of the Transcendent Function" for which I am doing a good bit of preparation. The course begins January 8th and runs for five successive days through the 12th. There are three hours of lecture and discussion each day, so all this preparation must be done in advance. While this is strenuous, it is also enormously interesting. I chose the subject matter myself because *so doing allows me time and motivation for a more thorough study of the material of the title, plus the three great metaphors Jung used to describe his inner process (that of Gnosticism, Alchemy and the Christian Mass). I thought long and hard about what I wanted to say to an august body of theologically-minded scholars, and decided I would risk an account of my own spiritual journey.*

As I grow older, I find it less comfortable to participate in active church life, yet I still search for a way to celebrate Eucharist. So now I attend a "High Church" Anglican service, very old formal style, and I like to sing the Gregorian chant with the old monks. The theology is fearful, but the spiritual mystery of the Mass, somehow, remains manageable when it is sung. So it is, for me, that way the aesthetic mystery is maintained and one can become like the marsh hen in the watery bog, just singing along for the joy of it. This is like the way the old monks sang every day, for hundreds of years, up at the Monastery at Einsiedeln near you.

Maybe they still do!

Such serious thoughts! I would wish to come and talk with you once again in person, perhaps in the spring, if you are still willing to receive visitors.

Warm best wishes, Mary Dian

I called Franz on November 27 to wish him happy birthday, and we visited on the phone. At first there was no answer so I rang Els who said she was not too well—trouble with her heart and with indigestion. She told me that for his birthday the next day, Franz invited his family to Hotel Sonne for dinner, and they will then attend Don Giovanni in Zurich. A short time later, Franz rang me back and we talked. He said his health was good although he tires more easily. He and Els continue their walks for an hour each day. "We stop to look at the sky or the fields and woods, or the stars depending on the time. There we are, an old couple."

He mentioned how difficult his birthday is as it coincides with the anniversary of Emma's death, Lilly's death, and their anniversary. He said, "We all lived here, and they are all still here, especially in the winter at night when it is dark and warm inside. When I assemble the living family, they do not know whether to celebrate or mourn or pick up the strands of history," he added.

With that, he said goodbye and rang off. I sat for a time with the phone against my ear.

Dear Mary Dian,   *February 11, 1992*

Both Els and myself send you greetings and thanks for your recent letter.

We are both not exactly in good shape, on and off in Hospital, since new years beginning, both with heart troubles or circulation troubles. First me just on 4th Dec. then a fortnight later Els, both not ill but the doctor thought it wise to control my low blood pressure etc., and Els had since long had rather undefined uneasiness and pains in or around her heart, so she had to stay in beautiful hospital Männedorf for 10 days. She liked it very much because of the beautiful view over the lake toward the mountains, the very good care you get and the reassurance good doctors can give to the patient. We both are decidedly growing older, weaker, farting here or there loudly. Nothing severe or dangerous. Diagnosis had to be given out, but one has to take certain precautions and organize the day with a little more patience, being conscious that we are no more 30 y.

I hope we both can live with this, and we plan to go for a fortnight, beginning 8 March to sites in Engadin as we did the last five years. Walking or better skiing over the frozen lakes is such a freeing movement in the crisp, dry air and the normally all blue sky and warm sun, we would be very sorry if we had to carve out this!

Now, dear, Mary Dian, I am coming to your project of an article or book about my mother, my father or me. It is all impossible from my view of the problem.

I think you could use your journalistic ability for some thing in reality in reach for you, or, and which is really of a general need and interest.

As I told you, about my mother's life and personality is really very, very little known or published. I agree, her life beside such a man like my father was an adventure and a great luck because mother was most probably the only woman with whom my father could manage his life and she to develop her own personality from school girl and innocent Miss to a ripe and experienced woman, knowing also the wider shores of life.

As there is so little known, I could see no one than one of her children, all her lifelong good friends have died who could handle such a theme, but she should be a poet, a dramatist, and psychologist, we have nobody with all these qualities.

About Father was and is written, filmed, TV, etc so much, that all is already said and written many times. You never could add more to his life portrait.

My life is just too uncomplicated to say much about it. Everything happened as normal as possible and I was happy to choose my works after my own wishes and possibilities, to earn money with my profession was happily a second or third motif and never a need! As I was not every ambitious, I had a happy life professionally and being the son of C. G. I had all the time learned a little to handle the discussions, misunderstandings and make good again with my dear wife and children. I would have all the difficulties to remember my facts of life even if I were interested to go back in previous times. And then I think that my person is for nobody an example how to live life.

If I were not the son of C. G. nobody would ever turn around because of myself. All my works and all what I did besides, I have done for private people and very rare for instance for a school or for industries.

Here comes Els into my living room full of music by a Mozart adagio, greeting me with "du bist schon der ungewohnlichte. Mensch!" This because I am giving answer to your letter and we discussed earlier in the afternoon about the situation.

Why do you want to write about somebody else, why not about your own thoughts? You have had quite a long life! I bet far more has happened in it, which might interest a general reader. When I think about your singing for the water birds! Your experience in educational problems, in schools, etc, is important for our present life of your children and your country and I mean this would give enough material to publish out of your experience of life!

Because of my life, neither Küsnacht, nor Switzerland, nor Europe or foreign countries would use one drop of ink nor read more than a line!

With such a state of things I am happy, because I know from little compliments that my clients of 30-40 years ago are still loving their houses, and are happy to sit at their chimney fire remembering the hours of discussions with their architect.

Recently I was invited by an old lady, who is living in a house of mine. She mentioned this and that and she had a bad conscious not having asked me before, but when I approved her changing and was appreciating her new ideas, she was very happy and I too, because I saw that my house, earlier drawn for a six people family, now had to fulfill new necessity for one old lady with occasional visits by her grandchildren, etc., and the house was still good and suitable for such new purposes. For me such reactions are far more gratifying than public honour or notice. Whenever you return to Zurich, you know that you will have a warm welcome and a roof over your head.

I am sure we, Els and myself, would find all the pleasure to see you again.

With kindest regards, Franz & Els is sending her love to you . . .

Dear Franz,   April 25, 1992

I have struggled long and hard to come to an answer to you from your last letter to me, in which you spoke of yourself as not important. There is a long letter to you, here on my desk, written shortly after hearing from you, which I have never quite had the courage to send. And so I have been in a state of suspension, unable to articulate the power and passion of my own faith in words. All along these months there has been a growing desire to try to reach you with something almost ineffable regarding my own faith or what C. G. would only term "the numinous."

Last spring I was invited, along with Warren, to share a lecture format, the annual "Jungian Lecture" to be presented to the faculty and student body at St. Paul's Theological Seminary, here in Kansas City. St. Paul's is a distinguished seminary, more specifically "Liberal Methodist." I thought long and hard about what I wanted to say to an august body of theologically-minded scholars, and decided I would risk an account of my own spiritual journey. I'm sending a tape of that presentation to you in hope that you might understand my process, and perhaps your own "slow wanders in the sun" to some degree. Mostly I send it to you in the hope that it might re-kindle in you some of the richness of dialogue we have shared in the past. There are some strong pulls for me, to return to Küsnacht this coming fall. I need to spend time with Helmut and Eleanor Barz who were tutors for me in psychodrama, now that my own practice encompasses several groups working in this mode. the second is to spend some hours with Toni Baker, who was my own analyst while I was last in Zurich and whose wisdom and insight I need to call upon once again as I work with my own clients. The third is, of course, a desire to spend some hours with you and Els. I hope to come in the early fall. Please let me know what is in your schedule, and when you will be available for a visit from me.

Fondly, Mary Dian

Dear Mary Dian,   *November 10, 1992*

I am very sorry to tell you that Els passed away Nov 5. in hospital. She had a deadly heart attack and died in minutes. Only the night nurse was with her, and I had dined 3 hours before with her in her room in hospital in a relaxed and easy giving atmosphere!

Though she had some warnings (dreams) before we did not thought that death is just standing at the door.

I feel very lonely, it is for me a big loss! Good by and take care.

With kindest regards, Franz

Dear Franz,   *November 17, 1992*

I am writing this letter in honor of Els, your dear companion, in an effort to join you in your grieving, which must be inexpressibly difficult to bear. After receiving your letter yesterday and talking with you by telephone, I was relieved that I was able to have the remainder of the day free enough to enable me to be alone in my study to play the Schubert Mass and give attention to my own favorite recollections of Els who has been for many years your partner and dearest friend. That you must bear yet another so great a loss in impossible for me to fully comprehend, Franz. I can only think of what the loss of my beloved Warren would be like, and I can scarcely fathom such a pain in the heart. It was my privilege to see something of the depth of your relationship with Els first-hand, and to comprehend the enormous pleasure you brought to one another and the tenderness you shared. This was a rare and lovely thing.

In my time of solitude yesterday, I gathered the things which Els had given me together at my desk. The letter inviting me to her home, several photographs, and the lovely glass piece of Küsnacht art which catches the afternoon sun at my window. I placed the photo of you two, sitting under the white cow painting, alongside your notice in front of me to aid me in my own memories.

I recall the day you took us to Bollingen, which was my first meeting with Els, who quietly lent me her warm spirit of friendship. How kind she was, and so sensitive to all that Bollingen is, particularly to you. She told me that she, too, loved to come there and feel the mystery and power of that house and woods. How kindly she smiles in my mind's eye as I recall that sparkle of sweetness in her eyes. And how sensitive she was to my own quest. A year later, she met me at the airport and we drove through the early springtime to Küsnacht in her little car with the oriental rugs on the floor. She spoke then of her sister, and her own plans to visit and comfort her later in the week on the anniversary of the death of her sister's husband. I recall what fun we had with our little dinner party for Elton and Ella Squires, shopping and planning together like young girls. How she enjoyed bringing out her fine pink table linens and very best china and crystal with the real pleasure of setting a table that only a gifted hostess with a genuine gracious spirit knows. There was a moment when we were working together in the kitchen when she stopped, stood still, and said to me, "I like how you are in this kitchen," and we laughed and she gave me a warm hug, understanding something of our common bond in loving to entertain friends. That was such a wonderful evening! How courtly and handsome you were, pouring the wine and entertaining the guests with humor and style. And how Els smiled over the bouquet of white tulips Elton and Ella brought. I recall how she praised my Jambalaya and my slightly garbled bananas foster attempt when the flambé failed to flame! But it was good, nonetheless.

I recall how Els loved all flowers and kept them in her apartment at all times. One morning we walked in her garden and exchanged German, Swiss and English names of the beauties. That was the morning she took me to the fence and introduced me to Christoph's dogs who so warmly wagged for us.

Thursday morning, Laurie came to visit and share her book on 20th Century art with us. She was very relaxed with me and not at all shy about my being an American, for which I was pleased. She later wrote me a kind letter. After she left, Els prepared a special lunch of smoked salmon, delicious bread, cheese, onions, and capers. A rare treat! At that meal, she spoke at length of her life, her husband, home, Lilly's illness, and her sadness to have not been able to have children. She shared early photographs, one I recall of her and her husband in evening dress, looking very smart indeed. I recall also discussing the analytical process and how it sets people apart from one another... how that bond was for Lilly and Lorenz... and I recall thinking that Els herself had a very sensitive understanding of C. G.'s work and his contribution to the world. I was also aware of how she encouraged you to carry on your hospitality to so many who came to your door. She was quite a partner to you in that important task. At times, yesterday, I sang along with The Mass *for her. Benedicimus, Gratias agimus tibi. What an amazing reach-across-our-two-cultures she extended to me Pectate Mundi. Gloria in Solis sanctums.*

Ah, what your loneliness must be for her. Agnus Dei…pecatate mundi.

Els lived as long as her frail heart and beautiful spirit could live, Franz. I will never forget how quickly I learned to love her, and how grateful I am to have known her.

Thank you for letting me share my memories of her, and place them alongside yours this day. While mine are only brief and yours are bountiful and of a profound and highly personal nature, I bring them together with all humility.

I do not know how to help you in your loss. The solstice approaches, friends and family will be with you to share. And I know Els's spirit guides you in each day's tasks, which require that one foot goes before the other.

Somehow, I think of you finding the stone for your father after Emma's death, and waiting for him to be able to pick up his hammer and chisel. Perhaps such a time will come to you as well, somehow. I pray so. In time.

Donna Nobis Pacem. Amen

Fondly, Mary Dian

P.S. I spoke to Ella by telephone to tell her the sad news. She was so sorry to hear. It was a comfort to me to talk with someone here who also knew Els's warmth and energy. That was when my own tears found their way, when Ella said, "I know you loved her."

Dear Mary Dian,   *February 12, 1992*

Yours is a perfect letter of condolence. It could not be better. It was a nice idea of you to put as letterhead a photograph you took at Els's living room during your stay. I realize how much you enjoyed that visit years ago, and also how real you judge my relation with Els. She was for me, I was for her, so we lived in the last years, and I am very grateful to God that we had such a good time together. It is not so sure in my age to find a partner of such qualities after the much too early death of my dear Lilly, my wife. And even if you have the chance for meeting, it is not a matter of course that you understand each other as we did. We could give us both the necessary freedom and the warmth we needed in the right time. I am glad that you had such good memories for Els and that you liked her. The situation when she obviously approved your kitchen work, which was a big honor for you! First very nice and so typical for Els spontaneous reactions. You do understand me with my grieving, and you can feel what I have lost. That is quite enough to help me, more is not helping. Words do not bring consolation, much more the feeling of comradeship, going together, our memories flow together and accompany Els on her way from life to death. It will be a long way and a large stream of feelings, but I am sure she is held in it. Thank you for taking part in it.

At the moment, I am not seeing what is coming, what will make sense and how my life is again becoming useful to my surroundings. I have no more friends, some women "friends" much younger, mostly abroad, and my family around me. This is not exactly helpful, as I see mostly, that I need somebody who is looking after me, who is dividing his or her time with me, and leaves me a kind of duty of daily work I have to do. With Els we had it. No day passed without being in contact and our being had these and seemed to be useful.

At the moment, I feel rather that I am a burden, for myself, for my next in the house, though everybody is very kind to me. I am invited for walks, for lunch, to suppers, my grand-children come to me to ask or bring little things, etc. Even the big dog is one of them, entering the library to greet me, what before he never did. But all is not so inspiring. My fancy is not taken by anything. I am not engaged in any new idea. I know I cannot always look back to the time with Els, but I should look forward to new horizons. But where are they?

As I am a "non-believer" I know that help first comes from myself and only afterward eventually God will help you, so I follow one of my granddaughter's recommendations: "Don't give up Grandfather, keep to it, don't let go!" We will see what comes, what is flowing in my life's stream, what is washed on my bank.

Have a good time, be happy and safe and sound!

Kindest regards, Franz

Dear Franz,   *December 13, 1992*

Your letter greeted me upon our return from a week at our place on the ocean near Charleston, South Carolina, where Warren and I are blessed to spend four or five weeks intermittently during the year for rest and recuperation. There was a very high tide during our time on the coast. Our little place sits right on the ocean on one of the barrier islands, and we woke to find the tide perhaps only 20 feet from our doorway, which makes one a bit nervous. There is a small price paid, in anxiety, to live that close to the ocean's giant precocity. During our week there, I thought of you many times and even had an analogy in mind of the high tide, and how, as the forces of nature come so close, one fears being submerged and carried off. Your granddaughter is right – don't let go! I think also of your father's image, and of which he wrote, of the Green Christ wherein he dreamed of a crucified Christ in the green-gold metal of alchemical transformation. The problem of being a "non-believer" has to do with theological definitions, Franz. Many years ago, I made a "leap of faith" into an identity with Christ as a symbol of transformation of the self. It came not out of a theological construct but out of my passion to make a personal connection with that which is totally, "The Other" – that which could lead me to those parts of my own soul, my own selfhood, where my consciousness balked at any church or collective definition of God. Since that relinquishment to the Christos, there has been, for me a way to pray and those prayers have never once been denied answers. Kierkegaard calls this the Leap of Faith.

I have functioned as an analyst, also, outside the collective imprimatur of what Jungian analysts, as a collective organization, decide what or who is "in" or what or who is "outside." It is the same for me with the Christian church. I need Christ, and he does not fail me. I study Jung, and he has never failed to lead me further. Fortunately, C. G. was not a "Jungian," and Christ was not a "Theologian."

For those of us who cannot do our own selfhood through collective models, the path to transformation is, as you said, first from self—and then to that awesome need where we address in honesty and humility our own pain, and offer it up to the "other." So be it. I can only hope that this is possible for you, too, at some point. Sans Lilly, sans Els, sans friends, sans family. Only you. In request. In need. In hope. Please forgive me if this sounds as if I am preaching—Oh, God forbid! I only know that you are a deeply spiritual and religious man who knows what the sacred Numen is, in your own world. God is enormously real to you. That essence is not defined, for you, by church. It need not be!!

I am sending along Jessie Norman's Christmastide on disk because when I listen to the exquisite feeling-soul of this wonderful Black woman, I am rocked in the cradle of the Divine Mother, and held like a baby in her voice. Her soul, and highly differentiated feelings, is without equal. My own most powerful passion rises with her in "Once in Royal David's City" and the "Amen." The others are also splendid for me. I only hope they reach you as well. Please do not feel you must respond to me, as the sender, out of your "daily duty to write letters." It is enough for me to know that her voice is in your house.

May the Epifhanus be with you, wherein the grief and sorrow of life lie beside new thing trying to get born. Advent to Epiphany.

Fondly, Mary Dian

P.S. I send Jessie Norman in hopes "she" (the feminine missing in Christian Theology) will comfort you. The Paraclete? St. Thomas called The Holy Spirit the feminine part of the trinity. That is why the Nag Hammadi texts were delivered to Küsnacht. C. G. knew there would be no hope for conventional Christianity without the feminine inclusion in the God-Head. What is outrageous to the church is essential to me, and perhaps to you as well. We stand at the edge. But God is.

Dear Mary Dian,   *December 7, 1992*

All my best wishes for the coming Christmas-days and hoping that the New Year will bring to the world some better days than we had anno 1992. Just some two days ago, I had a parcel from Kansas-City with a CD record with Jessie Norman singing Christmas carols, incl. Stille Nacht....I think that this gift comes from you, many thanks for this nice surprise. It is astounding that such a singer, with this world famous marvelous voice, is singing all these simple but deeply moving melodies, traditionals, all over the country. This is a most welcome gift now, as it brings me old times when we used to sing under the Christmas tree, or even before in the village from house to house to get some Christmas cookies!

Now my grandchildren are playing with instruments, Susan flute, Joplin piano, but singing is no more in use, as nobody has a voice, not even the aunts of Susan and Sophie, who are school masters. But they accompany sometimes with recorder—flute.

On the 25 and 26 I normally am invited with my other sons, but this year till now nobody has said something. It may come.

I wish you a very quiet and peaceful day.

Kindest regards, Franz

After this, I backed off for a while as it seemed best to allow Franz the time and space to pass through the Christmas season unencumbered by any other conversations about Els. He had said nothing about the funeral, but I knew he still grieved her, and so in mid-January I wrote to him again and asked if he would be available for a mutual grieving session. We arranged a time of 10 A.M. Kansas City time / 6 P.M. his time. We agreed to be grieving together however we worked with it. We chose Yoyo Ma playing Bach as that was one of El's favorite pieces and gave ourselves an hour, and wrote whatever occurred to us. We did not share what we had written, but Franz did send a note saying, "Yes, a very good way to do mourning."

The last time I talked to Franz was in November of 1983 when I called to wish him a happy eighty-fifth birthday. He said he was still reading the daily news and answering some correspondence, but when he tries to read for very long, he falls to sleep. His friend, Frau Haggenback, invites him to join her on walks with her dogs. She has three children, although a son died ten years ago. He said Christoph's younger daughter is studying in Switzerland, and Karl is in Lausanne studying modern history and French.

He then told me the previous August he had visited England with Francis and they drove to Cornwall. Franz's mother had worked on the Grail legend and so he climbed up Tintagel in Glastonbury, Merlin's home, but it made him tired. They went to London after Glastonbury, but since he didn't feel well, they flew back after a fortnight.

I told him about my family and how we were going along and mentioned a workshop I'd participated in on Böllingen. Franz said his son Andreas was making photography archives for Böllingen. He said two sisters had come for tea yesterday and recalled wood chiseling, cupboards high up, things his father made seventy years ago. He remembered his father sitting on the veranda of the summer house, chiseling, carving, dragons, devils, and snakes—symbols. It was a lovely conversation and my memories of Böllingen were once more revived.

The last full letter that came from Franz is dated over two years before the event of his passing.

Dear Mary Dian,   *December 20, 1994*

I thank you very much for your thoughts and greetings for the coming Christmas and the New Year.

We will have a quiet "festival." It is more a day of memories of the years and my Dears I have had to leave behind, so my feelings are rather engaged and touched by all those uncontrollable happenings that life is serving through us through more than eighty years. Yes, when I was a young man, all my thoughts and my wishes were directed ahead, upward, chasing after ideals or ideas sometimes not to be realized. My grandchildren are in this stage, and when I am talking with one or the other, they can listen to me telling how I was in older times, and comparisons to our present times. They begin also to realize the problems of modern times, and the wishes, although they are still likely to see the problems, social, religious, moral, and think about it. They have to carry their burden earlier than I had in my youth, thinking that the whole world is on my own disposition! I am not enthusiastic at all.

I accept that the coming year is one more way toward the end, or better the gate to eternity of a spiritual life, and such ideas are always around in my head now. At the moment it is astronomy, the question where do we come from, and where are we going, which has my full attention. So I am very glad the Hubble telescope has been repaired, and I hope with success! I wish your family, your husband and children very good year ahead!

Love and greetings, Franz

Dear Franz,   *August 24, 1995*

It is always a pleasure for me to think of you, and a sorrow that I am not a better correspondent.

As you must know by now, I much prefer to talk by telephone, or face-to-face with my friends. I must tell you, however, that I hope this letter finds you in good health and well-being.

This year marks my 65th birthday, and I am due some acknowledgment of a celebrative accomplishment that I have attained such a distinguished seniority. In America, the age of 65 entitles one to think of professional retirement, which is far from my inclination, and the several acknowledgments bestowed by our government, such as freedom from carrying personal health insurance, and also freedom to use tax sheltered funds for personal use without taxation penalty.

When my dear husband became 65 two and a half years ago, we decided to close our counseling center, which Warren and a colleague developed many years ago, employing seven therapists and maintaining expensive facilities, He moved his practice to a private office and comfortable accommodations for only his practice, and I continue my work in my own home office. This proved to be to our advantage since we did not have to maintain a large support staff, equipment, etc. While this transition was somewhat difficult, he is now free to do his own work without being responsible for a large staff.

We celebrated his 65th birthday with a wonderful two week house party at our ocean condo off the coast of Charleston, South Carolina, inviting many friends and relatives to join us in celebrative activities. It was a grand party. Over the two week period, 35 people joined us (but not, of course all at once). During the second week, we had all children and grandchildren with us along with many friends, and there were sufficient musicians gathered to develop a lively string quartet. We had a grand finale with a dinner cruise off the Charleston Bay and a concert. You know that I, as a cellist, had a wonderful time. All of this celebration helped Warren adjust to his new status with more available time for his soul-live, writing poetry. He has since produced another fine book of poems, soon to be published.

So now it is my turn for an expansive celebration. For a while, I thought I would be spending a month in China, working with the Neuropsychiatric Institute at Nanking on expressive therapies. While the invitation to do so seemed to be an option I "should" seriously entertain, my heart was not really in it. This past month, that option closed due to reasons beyond my influence, and now I am free to set my own course. Today I wrote the C. G. Jung Institute in Küsnacht requesting information regarding the course offerings for the Spring Semester which begins January 15th. What I would do is come to Küsnacht and spend some intensive work on Fairy

Tale literature. I have begun to develop, in addition to my practice, a new method which involves a well-developed skill from years back, related to my work in Psychodrama.

So it is possible I shall be in Küsnacht from January through March in this pursuit. To take this time away from my practice, home, household and husband, felt at first to be impossible. But as Warren and I considered it, this is not only possible, but absolutely correct, well-deserved, and entirely appropriate. I feel, as I think of it, rather like how you must have felt when you realized the possibility of sailing the Andromeda in the Mediterranean Sea! And I am, as a ship under full sail, ready to claim whatever expansive waters may present themselves.

My chief concern is how this possible absence will affect my practice, and I ponder this issue daily, person by person, like a mother hen clucking over her dear brood. Nevertheless, the wind is set in motion and fills my lungs.

My extroverted intuitive nature leaps forward into the realm of possibility all too quickly. And I am even in hope that I might rent, from Jecklin, as fine as the instrument I was able to rent from them in 1988. I had an "altes dench" and "old one" those few months. A superb cello. I really wanted to purchase it and bring it home but could not take on the expense at that time. I really like playing an instrument in which much music has already lived before my hands are upon it. We do not have many resources for fine old instruments here in Kansas City.

With fond regards, Mary Dian

CHAPTER ELEVEN

CLOSING REFLECTIONS

✺

IT CAME TO ME EARLY IN MY FRIENDSHIP WITH FRANZ JUNG THAT this usual task of young adulthood might be particularly difficult for one whose introjection is coming from "genius" in the eyes of the contemporary world. I know those of us who practice psychotherapy encounter such questions daily. The questions may go something like this:

"Who am I, then, if the world thinks of my father (or mother) in this manner? What are my own gifts? Talents? Strengths?" It seems to me that one's own sense of "self" might either underestimate abilities, or quite possibly overestimate them in a manner that could be quite confusing. I must admit that this question, as my friendship with Franz grew, stayed with me. I have no answers, but it seems to me, from what I know of Franz's history, that there was an attempt, when he was eighteen years old and ready to find his own self-discoveries and enter training and preparation for his career; he discovered that medicine, after the first year and a half of medical school, was not for him.

I recall him telling me, "I needed to separate myself, some, from my father." We never discussed this part of his life, but the story is here, which he and his friend Els Glasser shared with me. Yet I knew that this was a great turning in one sense, but also like coming to a sign on a road that simply said, "Way." One does not ask why. One just turns and maybe says, "Oh."

One thing I do know: Carl Jung deeply loved this person who knew this himself. But I sensed this was all there was for him to say, and I asked no questions. I consider this story of the household and family history, as my friendship with Franz grew, to have been his way of trying to articulate, for me, that story, and trusted me to know something of the causes, changes, pleasures and pains, however he wished to share, might have occurred and developed.

I also know that in my practice, as I work with people, finding out who one "is" in the world sometimes includes a certain amount of trial and error, and I think only then are decisions made. One is apt to either overestimate themselves or underestimate their future or value in the domain of self-esteem. One comes across people who are apt to over or underestimate themselves as they approach adulthood, and certainly discovering their parental positions enters into their own factoring as these discoveries and decisions are made. Through my practice, as my thoughts developed as to how people learn to consider their own lives, who and what they are, and making career choices, I have no voice to add or end this thought process. But I do know that Franz spent the later years of his life, after both parents were gone and his boys raised, by returning to the family home with one visible ambition: to be of service to his father's world as best he could, and he did so with great respect. This seemed to be a contract that suited him, given his social and generously extroverted skills, well indeed.

In my retelling the story of Franz in my life, it seems the "why" question has remained, and in each day of my life, it seems to resonate.

There is another piece, which glows in the dark now, with two channels. The first is the vase. The reader will recall my encounter with the vase, perched on the shelf in Carl Jung's library; my response to it on my first day of meeting Franz drew from me and him some sort of bond, as if the shattered vase, once more made whole, was a beacon.

The second is the thing that has kept me at this tale and would not let me leave it; it is the one word that unlocked in me a veritable flood of memories and feelings in response to Franz, and that is the word "Stuttgart." Franz told me, during my second trip to Küsnacht, that he had changed his earlier plans of becoming a physician and went to Stuttgart to study and become an architect. Stuttgart is where I, too, discovered significant things about myself as a seventeen-year-old girl. I was the daughter of an officer in the American Armed forces, living in Stuttgart after it had been bombed mercilessly in World War II, nearly every large building left in shatters, except the marvelous Opera House where I fell in love with classical music and spent my weekends at the Opera. I recalled that when I first heard the word Stuttgart from Franz, I wanted to hear his story about the city. So we both had an experience in common, although his Stuttgart was some twenty years older than mine. We both deeply loved Stuttgart and were there at powerfully exciting years of our lives. My calculation is that young Franz, born in 1908, might have been somewhere between seventeen and twenty when he lived in Stuttgart. I do imagine the city seemed wonderful and full of hope. What was born new and shining for him in Stuttgart, bloomed for me there, too, as I developed plans and practices regarding two things: one, writing my weekly columns about people and their stories; and two, receiving a taste of encouragement at the opera house in Stuttgart to plan for a career in classical music as a singer. That was nourished by the great baritone singer Max Roth, who was my voice teacher for only a month before we had to leave Stuttgart. As a younger man, Herr Roth had even sung as a visiting guest at the Metropolitan Opera in New York.

Franz Jung and I had experienced enormous self-discoveries about our future while spending time in that city. There we pondered our lives, which required leaps onto unknown paths and parts of ourselves in a city new to us, unknown, fascinating, and loaded with new challenges. Of course, this happened to each of us, separated in time by something like twenty years.

I left Stuttgart desolate and disappointed and alienated from paths upon which I had ventured, in love with a city almost completely destroyed by bombing during the war. I promised myself I would help clean up the dreadful mess of destruction caused, in my own adolescent mind, by Americans like me. Instead, I felt I was the one who also got nearly destroyed. The fact that Franz and I had experienced almost violent changes in our late teenage years made me excited to know his story

Franz only began the study of his father's work after C. G's death. However, he was willing, and even eager, to participate in his father's legacy in several ways: particularly, inviting inquiring people to the house and maintaining an exhaustive correspondence as a guardian, if you will, of what JUNGIAN THOUGHT represents in the outer world order. He quickly discerned the serious students from the banal or curious ones, and genuinely strove to be whatever help he could be to the former. And this was done with a remarkable, gracious spirit. Though he read much of his father's work, he did not wish to join the corps of analysands that other members of his family had chosen to do.

It was my experience, certainly, that he served his father's world in his own way and with remarkable grace. I am speaking from my own experience, which remains in deep gratitude for this experience and hope that I have conveyed this in a useful manner. I must also express that Franz found his lady friend, Els Glasser, a great helper in this task that he undertook in my own case, and I am sure of others. It is also my hope that the friends and family of Franz Jung, as well as those who maintain the practice of Jungian thought and psychotherapy, find his story helpful. But . . . this experience with Franz has never left my mind, so I am taking a shot at this question that remains in my mind regarding my friend.

I have written that Franz and Els took me to visit and tour his son Peter's wonderful house that Franz had designed. There was one feature I had never seen before or since and have never forgotten. In the paneled dining room wall, just over the buffet, there was a stunning bas relief carved out of the paneling of a marvelous bowl of fruit. It must have been at least five inches in depth, each fruit a carved marvel. This was an unmistakable piece of simply gorgeous artistic skill. When I asked Franz from whence this work came, he nodded, acknowledging that it was his work.

The paneling wood of the wall must have been six inches deep, at least, on that side of the room. It was a splendid piece of design and workmanship. I am no architect, nor am I an accomplished critic of architecture, but I do know that I have never since seen anything like this in a dining room, and I know what a marvelous piece of art it was.

Ever since that visit to Peter's remarkable and beautiful house, my question remains: Did Franz understand what extraordinary art he had imagined and created? He must have. And he wanted me to see it. I have often thought our individual talents seem connected to locale or place, and personally travel with the owner of those talents wherever they may go. My father only sang when he was taking a shower or out on a lake in a boat with me early on Sunday mornings, as if the music in him was intimately associated with water. I only painted happily at my desk at home as a teenager in my spare time.

I wonder at what point in our lives we might find need for both privacy and solitude if our artistic talents become the source of our income or merely the source of personal pleasure, a "wool-gathering" like doodling. Somehow, perhaps, the art in us requires a specificity of time, space, leisure that moves only under certain conditions that may or may not even be totally conscious.

Of course, I know Carl Jung was a splendid artist as well. But his career was not his art work. He also knew about sculpture and created generously for himself alone, as if it were like breathing, each piece a dream symbol of the work itself. That same truth must have been part of Carl Jung's understanding of his paintings, as a part of the soul which can only be actualized by one's God-given talent. Was his skill less significant and important in his own mind? I guess we shall never know.

I asked Franz to please accept that his role in the history of Carl Jung was important, contrary to his ego position. And I must accept that this brings to full circle my own agonizing grief at leaving Europe in 1947. I am not trying to invent something of importance out of his life to justify my own need to finish something. The intuitive dear white horse led me, and us, along this bumpy and scattered path.

Franz Jung created beauty, in his houses and his carving, in his generosity to Jungian scholars, for others. But I wonder if Franz, talented architect and gifted artist, slipped away from the story of Franz Jung, even to himself. There are notes from admiring clients of Franz, people for whom he designed fine homes, and he was appreciated for efficiency, comfort, and careful planning. Sometimes I lay these fragments of Franz's story, along with my recall of him, together and wonder if his own genuine artistic talent and career seemed somehow insignificant to himself in light of his father's place in the world.

And maybe the little girl in my dream of so many years ago, who was so excited to be visiting the tower in Böllingen ... was ... is ... this same old lady FINALLY FINISHING THIS STORY, which, somehow, she just had to write.

The End

The Author

credit: Stephen Molton

After her retirement in 1983 from a full career as an educator and later an executive for the Public Broadcasting System, **Mary Dian Molton** began her Jungian studies and earned an advanced degree in clinical social work. She has studied at the C. G. Jung Institute in Zurich, has trained extensively in psychodrama, and has worked as a Jungian psychotherapist since 1987. She is the co-author (with Lucy Anne Sikes) of *Four Eternal Women: Toni Wolff Revisited—A Study in Opposites* (Fisher King Press, 2011). She holds a B.F.A. in fine arts and an M.S. in education with a specialization in secondary theatre education. For several years, she wrote, produced, and chaired a weekly television series that showcased creative teaching.

The Editor

Janet Sunderland is an actor, writer, teacher, editor, and spiritual counselor/healer, practicing the hands-on technique, Huna Lomi. She earned a B.F.A. at Kansas State University in Manhattan, Kansas, majoring in fine arts and theatre, an M.F.A. in the Great Books Program of St. John's College, and an M.Div. from Sophia Divinity School. She is a published writer, both in poetry and memoir, and holds a Screen Actors Guild membership. She has been interested in and has read the work of Carl Jung for many years. Her memoir, *From Ocean to Desert*, is forthcoming from Shanti Arts Publishing.

Shanti Arts

Nature ▪ Art ▪ Spirit

Please visit us online
to browse our entire book catalog,
including poetry collections and fiction,
books on travel, nature, healing, art,
photography, and more.

Also take a look at our highly
regarded art and literary journal,
Still Point Arts Quarterly, which
may be downloaded for free.

www.shantiarts.com

Lightning Source UK Ltd.
Milton Keynes UK
UKHW010724200722
406119UK00001B/287

9 781951 651701